CLEAN SWEEP™

CONQUER THE CLUTTER

RECLAIM YOUR SPACE, RECLAIM YOUR LIFE

TLC
LIFEUNSCRIPTED™

Meredith® Books
Des Moines, Iowa

CLEAN SWEEP CONQUER THE CLUTTER

Writer: Melissa Bigner
Senior Editor: Vicki L. Ingham
Designers: Chris Conyers, Jana Rogness, Beth Runcie, Joe Wysong (Conyers Design, Inc.)
Senior Associate Design Director and Photographer: Doug Samuelson
Copy Chief: Terri Fredrickson
Publishing Operations Manager: Karen Schirm
Senior Editor, Asset and Information Manager: Phillip Morgan
Edit and Design Production Coordinator: Mary Lee Gavin
Editorial Assistant: Kaye Chabot
Book Production Managers: Pam Kvitne, Marjorie J. Schenkelberg, Rick von Holdt, Mark Weaver
Contributing Photographers: Michael Jensen Photography; Tommy Miyasaki; Tim Murphy, Foto Imagery Ltd.
Contributing Copy Editor: Jane Woychick
Contributing Proofreaders: Beth Havey, Beth Lastine, Brenda Scott Royce
Indexer: Stephanie Reymann

MEREDITH® BOOKS
Executive Director, Editorial: Gregory H. Kayko
Executive Director, Design: Matt Strelecki
Executive Editor/Group Manager: Denise Caringer
Marketing Product Manager: Tyler Woods

Publisher and Editor in Chief: James D. Blume
Editorial Director: Linda Raglan Cunningham
Executive Director, New Business Development: Todd M. Davis
Executive Director, Sales: Ken Zagor
Director, Operations: George A. Susral
Director, Production: Douglas M. Johnston
Director, Marketing: Amy Nichols
Business Director: Jim Leonard

Vice President and General Manager: Douglas J. Guendel

MEREDITH PUBLISHING GROUP
President: Jack Griffin
Executive Vice President: Bob Mate

MEREDITH CORPORATION
Chairman and Chief Executive Officer: William T. Kerr
President and Chief Operating Officer: Stephen M. Lacy

In Memoriam: E.T. Meredith III (1933-2003)

TLC (The Learning Channel), TLC (The Learning Channel) logo, Clean Sweep, and the Clean Sweep logo are trademarks of Discovery Communications, Inc., used under license. www.discovery.com
Clean Sweep Book Development Team: Douglas Ross, Greg Stewart, Kathleen French, Dean Minerd & Sue Seide, Executive Producers, Evolution Film & Tape
Roger Marmet, Executive Vice President and General Manager, TLC
Terri Johnson, Executive Producer, TLC
Sharon M. Bennett, Senior Vice President, Consumer Products
Carol LeBlanc, Vice President, Marketing & Retail Development
Elizabeth Bakacs, Vice President, Creative Services
Erica Jacobs Green, Director of Publishing
Cheryl King, Publishing Associate

"PEOPLE SAY THEY HAVEN'T GOT TIME TO BE ORGANIZED, AND THAT'S SUCH A FALLACY. WE CAN'T AFFORD NOT TO BE ORGANIZED. IN THIS DAY AND AGE WHEN THINGS MOVE SO FAST AND HOUSEHOLDS ARE INVOLVED WITH SO MANY THINGS, BEING ABLE TO QUICKLY AND EFFICIENTLY ACCESS THE THINGS THAT YOU NEED TO LIVE YOUR LIFE MAKES LIVING STREAMLINED, EASIER, AND MUCH LESS STRESSFUL."

— *CLEAN SWEEP* ORGANIZER PETER WALSH

CONTENTS

PART 1 MEET THE TEAM
pg. 6

Tava Smiley	8
Peter Walsh	10
Eric Stromer	12
Molly Luetkemeyer	14
Angelo Surmelis	16
Kelli Ellis	18
James Saavedra	20
Behind-the-Scenes Buds	22
Do You Need the Team?	24

PART 2 WIPE THE SLATE CLEAN
pg. 26

CHAPTER 1 ASSESS YOUR SITUATION	**28**
Do You Need a *Clean Sweep* Quiz	31
What Clutter Costs	35
CHAPTER 2 SORT IT OUT	**40**
Sorting Tool Kit	44
Tips for Sorting	46
Keeper Quiz	47
Sorting Do's	50
Paperwork	53
CHAPTER 3 SELL YOUR STUFF	**54**
Yard Sale Tool Kit	58
Make It Fun!	60
Yard Sale Do's and Don'ts	63

PART 3 MAKEOVER TIME
pg. 64

CHAPTER 4 FUNCTION RULES — 66
Plan the Perfect Closet — 71
Before and After: Living Space — 72
How-To: Love Seat with Built-In Bookshelf — 76
Before and After: Office — 78
How-To: Desk for Two — 82

CHAPTER 5 DESIGN DICTATES — 84
Money Matters — 91
Before and After: Bedroom — 92
Before and After: Playroom — 98
Before and After: Rec Room — 102
How-To: Stacked Storage Units — 108

CHAPTER 6 PAINT IT PERFECT! — 110
Paint Tool Kit — 113
Show Secrets — 115
Before and After: Bedroom — 116
Before and After: Office — 118
Before and After: Playroom — 120

CHAPTER 7 FIT FURNITURE — 122
Eric's Easiest Builds — 126
Before and After: Office — 128
Before and After: Bedroom — 130
How-To: Monogrammed Pillow — 132
Before and After: Laundry Room — 134
How-To: Laundry Folding Table — 136

PART 4 ORGANIZE YOUR WORLD
pg. 138

CHAPTER 8 STORAGE — 140
Organization and Storage Tool Kit — 145
Before and After: Office — 146
How-To: Wall-Mounted Shelves — 148
Before and After: Garage — 150
How-To: Multipurpose Table with Shelf — 154
Before and After: Bedroom — 156
How-To: Curtained Doors — 158

CHAPTER 9 MESS MAGNETS — 160
Clothes and Closets — 162
Crafts and Scrapbooks — 164
Toys — 164
Books and Bookshelves — 164
Bills and Filing Cabinets — 165
Mail — 165
Shoes — 166
Miscellaneous Supplies and Drawers — 166
DVDs, CDs, and Videotapes — 167
Memorabilia — 167
Photos — 167

CHAPTER 10 KEEP IT CLEAN — 168
All for One and One for All — 173
Before and After: Bedroom — 174
Before and After: Playroom — 175
Before and After: Bedroom — 176
Before and After: Living Room — 177
Before and After: Office — 178

CHAPTER 11 LAYOUT TOOLS — 180
Furniture Templates — 184
Clean Sweep Grid Paper — 188
Index — 190

PART 1

MEET THE TEAM

Would you invite America into your home, even if you were embarrassed by it? Tough question. But each season almost 14,000 people apply to appear on the hit TV show *Clean Sweep*, all seeking the chance to sort through the clutter in their lives (and sometimes literally air their dirty laundry) in front of a national audience. They bare family secrets and invite a cast of strangers to run the show. So what gives?

For starters, it takes a special person to admit that his or her life has become unmanageable. And it takes equally special people to lend a helping hand. The *Clean Sweep* team is a trustworthy, warmhearted group that can set almost any clutterbug straight. So before you dive into *Clean Sweep* 101, meet the team that will take you from a messy life to a marvelous one.

CLEAN SWEEP

TAVA SMILEY

TRYING TO KEEP UP with host Tava Smiley is like trying to catch a train that's roaring past at top speed. On camera and off, she's all over the place, popping in and out of crafting, painting, and carpentry scenes with the rest of the cast and crew; teasing homeowners about the more peculiar items they've amassed in their keep, sell, and toss piles; and donning whatever yard sale costume is necessary to goad customers to shop till they drop. If chief organizer Peter Walsh is a good-cop-bad-cop combo, Tava is 100 percent cheerleader for everyone involved in the show. "What can I say?" Tava says with a throaty laugh. "I've always had a lot of energy." It's good she has, because her winding path has demanded it in spades.

Tava grew up in unpretentious rural Missouri. She went to the University of Missouri and planned to attend law school afterward, "but I kept finding myself involved in plays and acting on the side," she says. Tava eventually listened to her inner acting diva and moved out West to give show biz a full-time try. When she landed on *Clean Sweep*, she recalls, "My friends and family laughed and then asked if it was a joke." Why such a universal response? "My house, my car, my bags—they are all a complete mess! I'll save a smiley-face sticky note someone's left on my car. Once I even found something growing in the back of my SUV—what I had thought was a box of head shots was actually a box with an old pizza that had been there waaaay too long. What can I say?"

A SELF-DESCRIBED PACK RAT, Tava can relate to the homeowners on the show. "I get what they're going through because I've been in the same boat," she says. And she's reforming: "Being on the show has changed the way I do things. I'll shop but I don't just buy something because it's on sale or cute—it's got to have a purpose and place. And I'm hitting all the boxes in my house too, organizing one a week till it's all done." As for her car? "It may be a little messy," she says, "but at least it's not smelly anymore!" ⌂

> **"The most rewarding thing about being on the show is that we're part of something that really helps people."**

GET TO KNOW...TAVA!

My nickname as a child was Ricky Ticky Tava; my nicknames on the *Clean Sweep* set are Tavalicious, Tavalina, Tavacita, Tavis, Tavs, Tava Nagila.

When we're on the road for *Clean Sweep*, I make my hotel room more "me" and homey by filling the room with candles and the fridge with stuff from a health food store; unpacking; and creating a small mess.

If I could edit/change anything I said in an episode, it would be: I only get one thing?

I could never *Clean Sweep* my friends, family, and Moroccan mint lattes out of my life.

ORGANIZER

PETER WALSH

GET TO KNOW…PETER!

My hometown is Melbourne, Australia, but I tell people it's Mobile, Alabama—the accent gets them every time!

My sign is Virgo. This is relevant because we love order and attention to detail.

When we're shooting on the road, I make my hotel room more "me" and homey by taking my favorite family photographs and my pillow.

My home workshop needs a serious *Clean Sweep*.

I could never purge my artwork out of my life.

ONE MINUTE

he's lost in thought, waist-deep in a sea of clutter, hands on hips, brow furrowed. Then in a flash, an impish grin takes over, and he bounds over the piles like a kid, laughing at some exchange. A few seconds later he's back to earnestness, crouched over a box of photos, tenderly touching a homeowner's shoulder as he counsels letting go of a past that's robbing him or her of the present. And so it goes, back and forth for four to five hours straight, as organizer Peter Walsh plays a dual role of good cop/bad cop while leading another family of admitted clutterbugs through a *Clean Sweep*. The ultimate goal? To purge their hearts, heads, and homes of mayhem and mess.

The process is exhausting and intense, but Peter is driven about organization and will go to any length to help the participants—and viewers—liberate themselves. "At the very base level," he says in a still-thick Australian accent, "*Clean Sweep* is about throwing people a helping hand. I am there as an advocate for the family, as a crusader for them. But there's an inherent problem, as they have been self-destructive. So I have to hold up a mirror and let them see themselves and their situation in a different light, from a different perspective."

It works episode after episode because the man is a pro and because on-camera jokes and tough love aside, he's all heart and dead serious about breaking through. Such passion can't be scripted, and in Peter's case it has grown as he has followed a life path devoted to teaching. After studying elementary education and teaching in his native Australia, he became involved in health education and drug abuse prevention programs for kids and picked up a degree in psychology. "In Australia," says Peter, "drug prevention for children centers around developing strong interpersonal skills so they won't need to resort to drugs later. So there's a lot of work on personal development, self-esteem, conflict resolution, decision making ... You see the thread starting to develop?" he asks.

After stints with for-profit and nonprofit corporations, Peter eventually wound up at *Clean Sweep*. How? "I was helping with the casting of the show and was asked if I'd be interested." He was told the show was as much about people as about organization, he says, "and that's what got me."

PEEK AT ANY EPISODE and you'll see Peter completely absorbed with the family of the day. He's relentless for a reason: By tuning in to their words and body language and how they relate to each other, he's able to get to the root of the problem—what started and perpetuates the chaos in their lives. "That's how I got insight into their heads and steer them to where they need to be," he says. "They have to find their way out," he adds humbly. "I just lead them." ◗

> **"When people stop sorting through their things and they suddenly get it—when the light goes on—that's what fuels me."**

ERIC STROMER

GET TO KNOW...ERIC!

My favorite set prank has been pretending to work while still asleep.

My Helen Reddy memorabilia collection needs a serious *Clean Sweep*.

I could never *Clean Sweep* my family out of my life.

The first thing I'm dying to do after we wrap a shoot is go to Austria, put on lederhosen, and sing to the mountains!

The one thing I'd like people to take from *Clean Sweep* is to never, under any circumstances, operate power tools while wearing long, flowing scarves.

WELCOME to a typical conversation with *Clean Sweep*'s carpenter, Eric Stromer.

INTERVIEWER: How do you keep up your energy and enthusiasm on the show?

ERIC: There's one thing and one thing only: humor. When you pair a construction project with a time limit and a camera, you've got to have humor or you'll die.

INTERVIEWER: How about on-set naps? Rumor has it you snooze on set at one point every day.

ERIC: *Ahem.* I consider naps to be essential in terms of safety. If you're tired and using power tools, you have to walk away and take a little nap. The Spanish really have it figured out with the whole siesta thing—I'm just waiting for it to catch on in this country.

INTERVIEWER: *Hmm.* What did you want to be when you grew up?

ERIC: My first idea was a dentist. That parlayed into a TV career in that it necessitated I have healthy teeth and gums.

INTERVIEWER: You just made that up, didn't you?

ERIC: Yes, I did. I spent four years at the University of Colorado earning a communications degree, but I am a carpenter on a TV show. Go figure.

INTERVIEWER: Are you a clutter-prone person?

ERIC: You could call me a onetime clutter-prone person. Now, as a result of *Clean Sweep*, I'm an incredibly organized and pristine human being.

INTERVIEWER: I was told to ask about your car.

ERIC: My car? Oh, well, it's another story, a horrible place, still a horrible nightmare. You've got to have one part of your life where it all falls apart, you see, and that's it for me. I invite you to put on a HazMat suit and come ride as a passenger.

"I love the emotional transformation that takes place with the people who come on our show. It's so cool to see the impact on these people of what we do—and how what I build plays into that."

Born in Chicago, Eric learned to wield a pneumatic hammer as a kid and grew up doing projects alongside his dad. After college, Eric found his way to Los Angeles and ended up on a soap opera. When his character got axed in a killer earthquake, he fell back on a college summer job skill—painting—and the carpentry know-how of old. "I was living in Santa Monica and got this shopping cart," he explains. "There were five cans of paint in it, and I went door-to-door, asking if anyone needed work done on their places." From such humble beginnings grew a successful construction company. One day Eric went to meet a client who was at an audition. The casting director—for *Clean Sweep*, it turns out—quickly ushered the bewildered builder in for a screen test of his own. And that was that.

"IT'S REALLY STRANGE," says Eric. "I thought I was done with the whole acting thing, but here I am, back around cameras. Still, it's different—being able to use every aspect of myself for this job: my humor, my artistic sense, my carpentry skills; it's great how all of those things are meeting at this apex called *Clean Sweep*. And it just showed up out of nowhere, like all the great things in my life." ⌂

GET TO KNOW…MOLLY!

The title of my autobiography would be
Confessions of a Neurotic.

My sign is Aries. This is relevant because: I am as bossy
as you would expect from an Aries, which helps more
than you know on set.

The most curious thing that people don't know about me
is that my real name is Mary.

Clean Sweep has changed my life because I now know I need
to brush the back of my hair much more often!

MOLLY LUETKEMEYER

(that's Loot-kah-my-err) is fired up. The designer is talking about a bedroom she designed for a teen girl a while ago. "Her family used her space to store things," Molly says. "And she didn't even have a door. At 13 privacy is critical, and no door? That had to change. From the beginning, I was on a crusade for her."

As any *Clean Sweep* homeowner can tell you, having Molly as your crusader is a good thing. A very good thing. Why? Because Molly hits single-minded mission mode as soon as she steps on set. Following the show's decorating edict—to marry form and function in a budget-conscious design—Molly creates some seriously fun and funky spaces: boldly striped rec rooms with basketball goals; window coverings that hint of Bedouin tents; living rooms that double as nightclubs; and always, always, always, color that explodes off the walls.

"We're really about lifestyle makeovers."

Molly's no-holds-barred approach comes in part from her firecracker personality and also, perhaps, from the road that led her to design work. She grew up with her two sisters in Baltimore, where her flamboyant self gravitated toward acting and the theater. After working as a stage actress in New York, she moved to Los Angeles and got into TV and film. But, she says, the transition didn't sit well. After having had her run with the industry, she was at a crossroads. "I thought, 'What am I doing?'" says Molly. "It was time for some soul-searching." Friends started in with advice: "You come over to my house and you leave and the furniture is in a different position," one said. Another piped up, "In the middle of dinner you jump up and make everyone get hammers and hang stuff everywhere. Why don't you try interior design?"

After some initial misgivings, Molly came around and dived into the design program at UCLA. One degree, a few prestigious internships, and a killer job later, she formed her own business with a client base of Los Angeles' rich and famous. When magazines started heralding her projects and including her on their "Best Of" lists, she was approached for on-the-air designing.

Molly explains why *Clean Sweep* was her top choice. "The combination of design and organization appealed to me. The show serves such a purpose, and I like the fact that our goal is to make the homeowner actually love the end result," she notes. That goal is not always common in TV design shows.

HOW ABOUT THE END RESULT for that 13-year-old girl? The soft-spoken teen scored a room with a door and a work space where she could do her homework and her artwork. And a graffiti artist created a one-of-a-kind headboard emblazoned with her name "After the reveal," says Molly, "she came up and told me that it was cool, that I was cool. At that age, there's no bigger compliment!" ♠

ANGELO SURMELIS

JUST PLAIN NICE by nature, designer Angelo Surmelis is also terminally tidy. He gets very uptight about clutter—always has. "I'm not proud of it at all," Angelo admits sheepishly. "Even when I was little, I'd clean out and organize my closet and bedroom on my own. And when I was done in my space (here's the really embarrassing part), I'd go into my younger brother's always-messy room, clean it up, and redesign it too. Of course," Angelo laughs now, "he thought it was great and loved it."

Angelo's self-deprecating wit and easygoing manner are par for the course, on set or off. And while he's serious about his work, he doesn't ever take himself too seriously. Maybe, he says, that's because he's not a designer by education. "When I was a kid," he explains, "I always wanted to be an architect. But I realized I couldn't do the math." Thanks to that epiphany, he jumped into his second greatest passion—acting—and got a degree in theater. Angelo then hit the stage in Chicago and later in New York before eventually moving to Los Angeles.

Angelo's friends began to notice that every time they saw his apartment, it was painted a different color and the furniture was rearranged. At their suggestion, Angelo started to take interior design projects that came his way. If you peek inside his home now, you'll see ideas, projects, and wall colors that you recognize from the show. That's because Angelo tests out his clean, modern concepts on his own turf before applying them to *Clean Sweep* houses.

"I'M A HUGE BELIEVER in mixing things up," Angelo says. "I just don't believe there are too many absolutes or rights and wrongs." Perhaps that sentiment explains why so many *Clean Sweep* families warm to him so readily. It's a mutual feeling of comfort and respect, and Angelo delights in the exchange. "It really is a luxury to be able to work in a *Clean Sweep* family's space. What we're trying to do for them—marrying good design with organization—it's just so cool and so right." ⬛

> **"I love that being on the show allows me to work with people who never thought they could have a designer come in and help them out."**

GET TO KNOW…ANGELO!

When we're on the road for *Clean Sweep*, I make my hotel room more "me" and homey by rearranging the furniture.

If I could edit/change anything I did or said in an episode, it would be: Nothing—I'd make a fool of myself sooner or later, so why bother trying to hide that?

My brain needs a serious *Clean Sweep*.

I could never *Clean Sweep* my dog out of my life.

The one thing I'd like people to take from *Clean Sweep* is that "stuff" is not who you are.

DESIGNER KELLI ELLIS

GET TO KNOW...KELLI!

The title of my autobiography would be *SuperMom: Where Did I Put My Keys?*

If I could change anything I do on the show, it would be: I say 'I love it!' too much...but I always mean it!

My garage needs a serious *Clean Sweep*.

The first thing I'm dying to do after we wrap a shoot is to wash the makeup off my face!

The most curious thing that people don't know about me is that I have to close the closet door in my bedroom at night because of boogey monsters.

"WHEN I WAS a kid," says designer Kelli Ellis, "my mom told me to make my bedroom into a 'model room', and I mistook that to mean a showroom. So I spent hours and hours designing and redesigning it—you know, sofa in one corner, window treatments over there…" The laid-back mother of two laughs, "Let's just say I was an only child and a very busy one. My idea of playing dolls? I'd decorate the dollhouse for hours on end and not change their clothes once!"

Kelli is a born interiors maven. After childhood, though, she veered off the design track. The daughter of an Orange County, California, judge, she first studied marketing and advertising and then went on to law school. "What can I say?" she says now with a so-it-goes shrug.

Kelli designed spaces "unofficially" while in school, and when she finally opted to make it a full-blown career, her client base was nearly established. "Word of mouth had really built up the work," she says.

Kelli's success was no surprise to her friends and family; they know this neatnik has a house that looks like a showroom. "I can't help it," Kelli says. "I just like walking into something clean that happens to look like it's the third page of a magazine. But I'm not a robot or crazy about it, especially with my kids. They tend toward the neat side, but let's face it, everyone needs to be able to let it all hang out somewhere."

Kelli made the leap into television when an old law school buddy mentioned that *Clean Sweep* was casting around for talented designers. "I sent in a picture of myself and went in for an interview," she remembers. "And the producers asked me to send in any other tapes I had. I just laughed and said, 'Whatever you've got of me—that's it. I really am just a designer-slash-mom.'"

"When a homeowner asks, 'How did you know what I wanted?' it's just the best."

Despite her lack of TV experience, Kelli turned out to be a natural on-screen personality, and she's not a bit camera-shy. She also enjoys being backstage on *Clean Sweep*. "I'm the biggest junkie for any behind-the-scenes show," she says. "I knew that it would be fun and interesting just for that peek alone, but now that I'm here and in the mix of what's happening and all the people involved, I cannot tell you how great it is, how much fun we have."

KNOWN FOR HER SOOTHING PALETTES and luxe-on-a-budget rooms, Kelli loves unveiling the finished designs during the reveals: "I love that part! It's absolutely why I am on the show, and every last time I cry. Someone is always handing me a box of tissues at that point." Remembering episodes past, she gets all mushy and says, "There's just nothing like it." ⬧

JAMES SAAVEDRA

FOR THOSE at home tallying tear-jerker moments on *Clean Sweep*, designer James Saavedra has yet to score a dry-eyed episode. "Yep," he says, gushing with pride, "it's true." And for a man who says he'd like to do for design what Oprah has done for self-help, that's the best track record he could hope for. "Sure, I love transforming a space into something fabulous," James says, "but more than that, I love, love, love being able to enhance somebody's life through design."

As a kid his toys of choice were crayons and building blocks, his favorite pastime anything art-related. And when Mom let 8-year-old James choose his room color, "I agonized over three distinct shades of blue," he says with a laugh. "One was pale, one was medium, and one was a saturated color." As an adult James started out in acting, but a job for an interior designer made him realize that he could turn his personal passion into a full-time career. Three degrees later, James was doing yearlong projects for major Los Angeles firms and designing home goods. When he saw a classified ad for an on-the-air designer, he thought he'd give it a shot. "Getting on TV was a way I could reach more people," he explains.

> "When a *Clean Sweep* family first walks into their new space and I see that look of amazement spread across their faces...I know why I do what I do."

And reach them he does. He may tend toward a blend of the traditional and funky in his own home, but when it comes to working with a *Clean Sweep* family, his own preferences go on the back burner. "I want to take their vision and make that into a reality," James explains. "My goal on the show is to bring our homeowners and audience a level of design that goes beyond rearranging furniture and slapping paint up on the wall. Anyone can do that, but it takes a different effort to get an 'aha' moment from a place."

"THE IDEA," James continues, "is that when you walk into your home, into a room, you've got to have an emotional attachment to it. My goal is to elicit emotion from the homeowners, because if you can tap into that, you'll be successful every time." ⌂

GET TO KNOW...JAMES!

My sign is Aquarius-Virgo rising. This is relevant because I love creating—as long as it's perfect.

When we're on the road for *Clean Sweep*, I make my hotel room more "me" and homey by hanging art in the bathroom and lighting candles.

The first thing I'm dying to do after we wrap a shoot is to relax and draw a bath.

The most curious thing that people don't know about me is that I once changed my name.

The one thing I'd like people to take from *Clean Sweep* is that even clutter holds possibility.

BEHIND-THE-SCENES BUDS

All the chumminess that you see on camera is nothing compared to life behind the scenes. There's a whole lotta love going around any show taping, and enough mischief to make the set feel like summer camp all year long. As Tava says, "If I didn't know better, I'd think that anyone who works on *Clean Sweep* had to take an attitude test to get hired. There's so much fun on the set, storytelling, messing around, and a lot of laughter. It has to be like that, because with all of us traveling together, working long hours in tight spaces, we've got to get along. The nice thing is that everyone's got each other's backs." Here's a sneak peek at some of the wackier moments.

CLEAN SWEEP

DO YOU NEED THE TEAM?

If you think you might be a candidate for a *Clean Sweep* of your own, Peter challenges you to take an open-eyed look around your house...and a good look in the mirror as well. "Are you at a place in your life where you realize your material possessions are causing you more discomfort than pleasure?" he asks. "More dis-ease than ease?" The families who once called these messy spaces home 'fessed up and changed their clutterbug ways. If their old rooms look like your present-day house, you've bought the right book.

IF YOUR ROOM LOOKS LIKE THIS,

YES, YOU DO.

PART 2

WIPE THE SLATE CLEAN

Congratulations! Arriving here means you've taken the biggest step: You've admitted you have a clutter problem and you're ready to do something about it. With that huge hurdle behind you, it's time to roll up your sleeves and get to work to *Clean Sweep* your space.

Before you tackle a large space, such as an entire room, heed Peter's advice: "My grandmother used to say, 'There's only one way to eat an elephant—one bite at a time.' That's true of clutter too. It can be overwhelming, so you've got to start small. Begin with one countertop, one bedside table, one drawer, and work your way up from there." Here's how to get started, one bite at a time, one step at a time.

CHAPTER 1

ASSESS YOUR SITUATION

ASSESS: **YOUR SITUATION**

Clutter happens when possessions take over a space so that it's no longer clean, usable, or functional. That definition sounds straightforward enough, so why are so many people knee-deep in a messy home? Maybe it's because they've lived with problematic piles so long they don't even see them anymore. That's when it's time for a reality check. Take the time to walk through your most troublesome spaces and put them to the following tests.

LISTEN UP

Describe a room that you suspect needs a *Clean Sweep*. Do you feel buried by the mess in it? Do you feel as if you're suffocating in it? Do you feel you are drowning in it? As the *Clean Sweep* team notes, most people use very specific language to describe clutter—and it's all negative, because clutter robs a space of life. Take note of the words you use, and an honest picture of your room will surface.

CLUTTER OR JUST A LITTLE MESSY?

Peter, the prince of organization, may banish clutter with an iron fist, but he's not a complete despot. "We're all human," he allows, "and a little mess is OK, even healthy. But the question is, what level of mess are you comfortable with?" Ask yourself if the mess is controlling you. Is it getting in the way of the life you want to live? Everyone has a different comfort level, so put these questions to yourself and your family members and set up personal boundaries.

STUFF EQUAL TO SPACE

Here's one way to ground yourself in reality: If you have room for 100 books and you own 100 books or fewer, you're soundly clutter-free. But add one more book to the mix and you've entered Clutter Land. Why? Because what you own is out of proportion to the space you have. Take an honest assessment of what you have versus your storage and display room. For a clutter-free home, you'll need to keep your possessions below maximum capacity.

QUIZ

- ▶ Do you have trouble finding your clothes in the morning?

- ▶ Do you have trouble locating any other items in your home?

▶ ## Do you buy duplicate items because you can't track down the originals?

- ▶ Do you have to clear away items to create a clean surface before you can perform everyday tasks?

- ▶ Do you panic before people come to visit and rush around hiding the clutter?

- ▶ Do you buy sale items for the bargain, not for the need?

- ▶ Do you shop when you feel depressed, bored, or troubled?

- ▶ Do you buy things in anticipation of the future (for unlikely emergencies, dream hobbies, and so on)?

- ▶ Do you have things in storage (in the home or elsewhere) that you have not accessed, needed, wanted, or looked at for six months to a year?

- ▶ Do you feel your possessions own you rather than you owning them?

▶ ## Are you embarrassed to have people over?

- ▶ Do you refrain from entertaining or having houseguests because of the stuff—and the condition—of your space?

- ▶ Do your children make negative comments about the condition of your home?

- ▶ Are your children imitating your clutterbug habits?

If you answered yes to any of the above, take a deep breath.

As the *Clean Sweep* team says, these are all indicators that clutter has spun out of control. But fortunately, owning up to reality is a major step forward, and this book is loaded with solutions. So chin up and keep on reading to give yourself a *Clean Sweep* lifestyle makeover.

ASSESS:

DOES YOUR BEDROOM LOOK LIKE THIS:

Can you see the floor?

Do you have to move things before you can sleep on the bed?

Are you able to find clothes and dress with ease?

Is the closet organized and efficient?

Are your clothes properly stored and cared for?

What do you see when you look under your bed?

How does this room make you feel?

Is the wall color inspiring and soothing?

Do you sleep well in this room?

"HOW MUCH SPACE YOU HAVE IS THE ULTIMATE DETERMINATION OF WHAT YOU CAN KEEP." —*Peter*

OR THIS?

DOES YOUR OFFICE/CRAFTS SPACE LOOK LIKE THIS:

Are you able to open and close all drawers, containers, and closets with ease?

Do you know what's in all your bins, drawers, and filing cabinets?

Does everyone using this space have room to sit comfortably?

Does everyone have a clean work space?

Are office machines (phones, computers, copiers, printers) functional?

Does everyone have easy access to office equipment?

Is there a logical filing system?

Are crafts projects current?

Are crafts supplies essential, organized, and used regularly?

Are bins clearly labeled and easily accessed?

Would you feel proud to have clients, customers, or your boss see this space?

How does this room make you feel?

"CLUTTER IS STUFF THAT'S NOT ORGANIZED, NOT RESPECTED, NOT HONORED. BY DEFINITION, IT'S ABOUT POSSESSIONS OUT OF CONTROL. AND THAT IS NOT OK." —*Peter*

OR THIS?

WHAT CLUTTER COSTS

Dollar Cost

If you have a 1,500-square-foot house worth $300,000, every square foot in the house is worth $200. If you have a 10×10-foot room you can't get into because of clutter, that's a $20,000 storage room. In terms of monthly cost, you're spending about 7% of your mortgage on storage. Are the things in that room worth that much?

Time Cost

Over the course of a day, write down the time it takes you to find your shoes, your clothes, your keys, paperwork, addresses, and so forth. If you spend half an hour a day trying to find these "lost" items, that's 3.5 hours a week, 15.5 hours a month, 182.5 hours—or seven full days—a year. Clutter has robbed you of a week of your life, and that total doesn't factor in the anxiety or anger you feel while hunting for missing items and the time it takes to calm down after the fact.

$$\frac{\text{Total house value}}{\text{Total square footage}} = \text{Value of 1 square foot}$$

$$\underset{\text{(length} \times \text{width)}}{\text{Square feet of cluttered space}} \times \text{Value of 1 square foot} = \text{Cost of dysfunctional space}$$

DOES YOUR LIVING ROOM LOOK LIKE THIS:

Is your living room easy to navigate?

Can you see the floor?

Can you see the furniture?

Is this space guest-friendly at a moment's notice?

Is there enough open space to use this room comfortably?

Can you find CDs, tapes, and DVDs easily in this space?

Are you proud of this space?

How does this room make you feel?

OR THIS?

"THE WORDS 'ORGANIZED' AND 'ORGANIC' COME FROM THE SAME BASE WORD. SOMETHING IS ORGANIC WHEN IT LIVES AND BREATHES. SO IF SOMETHING IS NOT ORGANIZED, IT LACKS LIFE; IT'S SUFFOCATING." —*Peter*

DOES YOUR WORK SPACE LOOK LIKE THIS:

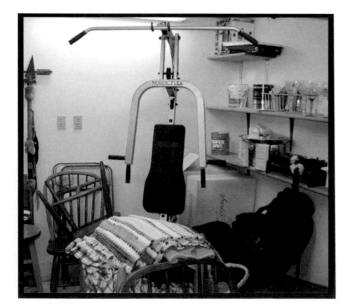

Is your work space safe for all who might use it (adults, seniors, children)?

Is dangerous equipment stowed safely?

Are work surfaces clear and is there sufficient room to complete tasks in this space?

Does everything have its place?

Have you maximized the space with vertical storage and shelving?

Are supplies labeled and logically grouped?

OR THIS?

"A CHARACTER IN A POPULAR MOVIE NOTED THAT IF YOU ARE NOT VERY CAREFUL, THE THINGS YOU OWN WILL END UP OWNING YOU. IF YOU HAVE A SPACE THAT YOU CAN'T USE BECAUSE OF YOUR POSSESSIONS, THEN YOU'VE CROSSED THE LINE. YOU DON'T OWN IT; IT OWNS YOU." —*Peter*

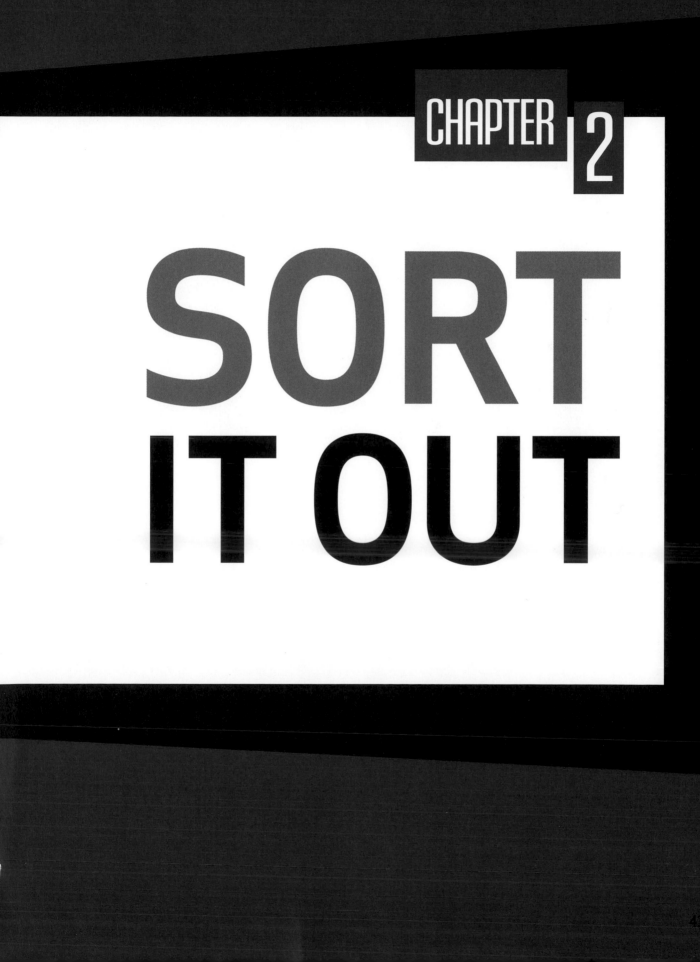

CHAPTER 2

SORT IT OUT

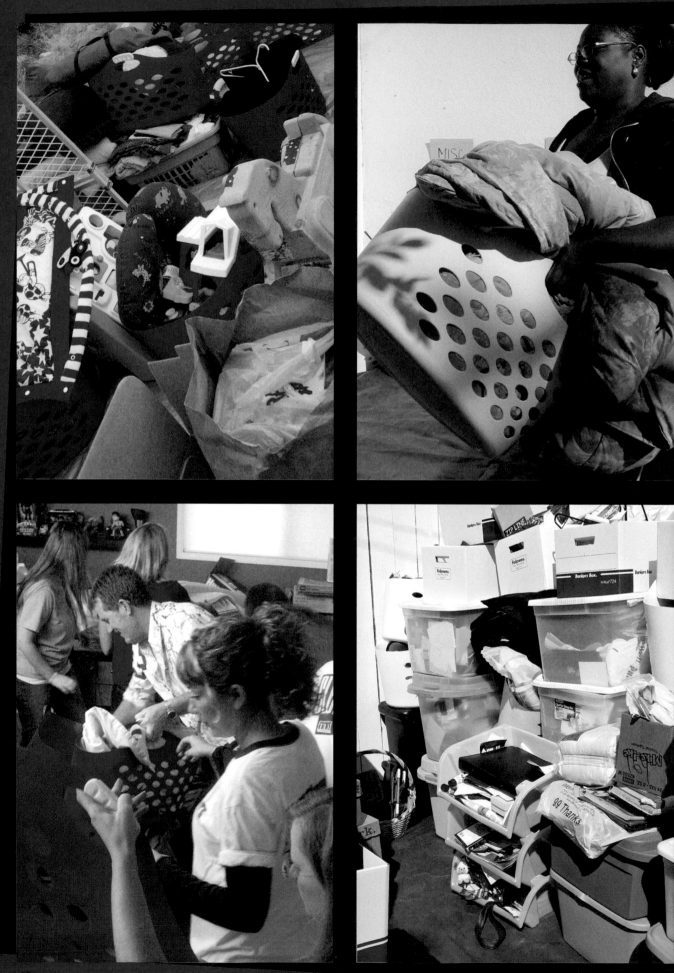

Welcome to the most intense—and most rewarding—step on the journey toward reclaiming your life and your living space. Don't worry—*Clean Sweep* will hold your hand through this process. But bear in mind this rule: How much space you have in your home will determine what you can keep.

Below: To conquer the clutter monster, it's essential to move everything out of the room so you can see how much space you actually have. The gorgeous wood paneling and built-in storage in this study were once hidden by piles of possessions. With the mess moved out, the homeowners could see the room's potential and fell in love with the place all over again.

STEP 1 PURGE

"Purge, purge, purge is the first step," says Peter. In other words, it's time to empty the space of its contents. "One of the big mistakes people make when . . . getting organized is that they go into a cluttered space and start organizing. That's a huge, huge error," he warns. It's also an expensive error if you buy new containers, files, and other organizational tools before you know which items you'll actually keep. So first turn the room inside out, emptying it of all it holds. Transfer the contents to a weather- and theft-proof space, such as a fenced yard or a garage. Placing items on large tarps is a good idea too, to protect them from moisture.

STEP 2 IMAGINE YOUR DREAM ROOM

Once you've purged the space, look around. Now you can actually see the room and its possibilities. Imagine how you want the room to look and function. Ask your family, your partner, your roommates—anyone who will share the space—to participate. It's important to agree on this vision as a team. Otherwise you'll be at loggerheads going forward, and any solution you come up with won't last. When everyone participates at the planning stage, everyone shares proud ownership of the project. That means people will be more likely to pitch in and help, and more likely to maintain order once the space is organized.

Above: Unusual horizontal paneling and a hardwood floor, unearthed from under piles of stuff, provide inspiration for a new room design.

STEP 3 DETERMINE ZONES

As you dream up your new space, ask yourself how you need the room to function. If you want it to be an office, an entertainment room, a game room, and a laundry room, you'll need to establish a zone for each of these functions. Zones come with a bonus: They'll help you decide which purged items can return to the space. For example, say a family room needs to incorporate three zones: a reading area, an entertainment area, and a work space. The reading zone necessitates a seating area with shelves for books and magazines. The entertainment zone needs storage for electronics (TV, DVD player, VCR, CD player), and for videotapes, CDs, and DVDs. And the work zone demands a desk, some storage for files, and possibly shelving too.

STEP 4 PLAN ORGANIZATIONAL SYSTEMS

Once you know what furniture each zone needs—a bookshelf, an entertainment center, a desk—consider the pieces you already own and decide whether any of them can serve the purpose. Also consider smaller storage pieces—drawers, baskets, chests—for orderly storage of DVDs, tapes, and CDs. What filing systems do you need for your paperwork? This is only the tip of the iceberg in reorganizing a space, but it's essential to have an idea of the organizational systems you'll ultimately need in the newly ordered room.

SORTING TOOL KIT

- ▸ Sturdy boxes
- ▸ Sturdy trash bags
- ▸ Paper shredder (see chapter 9)
- ▸ Tarps
- ▸ Wooden hangers
- ▸ Rolling clothes racks (or a sturdy clothesline) for "keep" clothes
- ▸ Sports drinks
- ▸ Snacks
- ▸ Sunscreen
- ▸ Babysitter
- ▸ Objective friends

Welcome to a top-notch *Clean Sweep* sort! The keep pile sits on brown and white tarps in the foreground; note how similar items have been grouped together in neat, sturdy boxes, and how books are placed spine-up for easy measuring and reshelving later. Everything you see here—and even more not pictured—rendered two rooms useless and took up more than 100 yards of this front lawn.

INITIAL SORT

STEP 5 SET LIMITS

Your zones determine what items can go back into the space—what makes sense given the function of each zone and what can actually fit into the organizational systems you choose. For example, if you have 20 feet of bookshelf space, and your books—measured spine-to-spine—are more than 30 feet, you must get rid of at least 10 feet of books. That's reality, and not veering from the truth is one of the biggest challenges you'll face while sorting…and one of the most liberating gifts you'll glean from the process.

STEP 6 SORT YOUR PILES

Now you've come to the heart of the *Clean Sweep* experience. Set up three piles: keep, toss, and sell. To get your feet wet without drowning, do as host Tava does and make a circle of your clutter mountain, warming up with big items. Go piece by piece and make a quick gut decision: keep, sell, or toss. Don't get bogged down at this stage or too stirred up emotionally. Take a short break after your first pass to take stock of your initial sort. If you've still got Pikes Peak to scale, you—and everyone pitching in—need to fortify yourselves and prepare to be tough. Have plenty of healthy drinks (like sports drinks or water) and snacks (like fruit or trail mix) on hand to replenish yourself during the process. Then go at that keep pile again and take the Keeper Quiz *opposite* for each item. If you get stuck, ask a trustworthy friend for help—and do what they say.

TIP 1 Set a time limit and stick to it. On the show, 20 to 30 minutes works well for the first stab at your keep pile.

TIP 2 "Think of the great state of OHIO—Only Handle It Once," says Peter. Pick up something and immediately place it in a keep, toss, or sell pile.

TIP 3 If you've got a box of things to wade through, put it in the keep pile for now.

TIP 4 Can't decide? Put the questionable item in the keep pile for now.

TIP 5 Place like items together in the initial and secondary keep piles. This will save time later.

What's a **SELL** item?

A "sell" is something you no longer need that someone else might find useful or collectible. "Sells" are also duplicates of keep items.

What's a **TOSS** item?

"Toss" equals trash, such as empty boxes, wrappers, insignificant newspapers and magazines, outdated calendars, broken toys, single shoes or socks, unsalvageable furniture, clothes, and so forth.

KEEP

KEEPER QUIZ

Ask yourself these key questions before putting an item in the keep pile.

▶ Do you love it?

▶ Do you use it regularly—at least once in the past three months?

▶ Is it being honored and respected?

▶ Is it dust-free?

▶ If it's clothing, does it fit you today?

▶ Does it work?

▶ Do you have the space for it?

If you answered yes to ALL of the above, it's a keeper.

STEP 7 ORGANIZE YOUR KEEP PILE

Before you load your cherished keepers back into your newly cleaned-out space, it pays to organize your loot. On set, the cast and crew always set up an area they call "Org World." Org World is a beautiful, orderly place where chaos is tamed with the following tools:

▶ Clothes-folding boards
▶ Wooden hangers
▶ Rolling clothes racks
▶ Tie racks
▶ Hat racks
▶ Containers for books, CDs, videotapes, and so on
▶ Desktop and office drawer supply organizers
▶ Clear plastic bins for shoes
▶ Label makers
▶ Photo boxes, photo albums, and photo frames
▶ File folders and filing systems

For details on how to organize specific mess magnets (clothes, books, crafts), see chapter 9. Learn how to fold clothes perfectly on page 145.

PARTNER UP

"Who's the person who would tell you your favorite sweat suit makes your rear look the size of Texas?" asks Peter with a grin. "This person loves you enough to tell you the truth, and you trust them enough to know they have your best interests at heart." Having an objective helper is essential when you're plowing through the piles of emotional baggage attached to your possessions.

A partner can guide you through the process, acting as part cheerleader, part coach during the sort. (If household members disagree on any item, this neutral party becomes the referee.) Pick a person with stamina and reward him or her for helping out. Peter even suggests that couples make it a form of entertainment. "Invite a couple over one night and all four of you go through one closet. Order dinner, play music, and catch up while working." Set a time limit at that house; then head over to the other couple's house for dessert and go through one of their small clutter zones. That way it's a social game rather than a solitary chore.

"My grandmother has said that you can go broke saving money," Peter says. So take a cue from granny and splurge a little when buying containers to suit your newly organized space. The *Clean Sweep* crew combs shopping aisles everywhere for the crème de la crème, checking out home goods, art supply, hardware, organizational, and discount chain stores for the perfect box to store whatever a homeowner needs to stash. They suggest you aim for sizes and shapes that suit your space, and looks that will inspire you to keep things clean.

At the end of each show, Peter often confesses that he has spent the bulk of his room makeover allowance on storage and organizational supplies. But he wouldn't have it any other way, as the investment pays off immeasurably. Good storage and organization improve the quality of life and reduce time spent on everyday tasks. That's worth a lot.

MAKING TIME

Time is one of the biggest hurdles to getting the ball rolling for a *Clean Sweep*. Try these ideas:

▶ Set aside a day that works for everyone involved—all the household members and your neutral third party. Make a backup rain date.

▶ Create a schedule with start and stop and break times so everyone knows that the process has an end.

▶ Can't do it all at once? Break it down into smaller bites. Tackle one area of the room at a time, one closet at a time, one shelf at a time. Still, set a time limit.

▶ Give yourself a public deadline. If you schedule a dinner party, you'll be forced to clean your now-cluttered dining room by that date.

▶ Advertise for a yard sale a week in advance; this will force you to purge your house before the event.

▶ Don't have time to tackle a whole room? Break it down into smaller pieces and devote a half day or as much time as you can to the space.

SORTING DO'S

SET SMALL SORTING GOALS. If you can't purge a whole room, purge a closet. If you can't purge a whole closet, purge a shelf, a drawer, or something doable.

TACKLE ONE TYPE OF CLUTTER at a time after purging a room. Start with big furniture; then work your way down to clothes, books, magazines, paperwork, photos.

GROUP LIKE THINGS TOGETHER when you empty a room and after you've sorted keep items.

GET RID OF DUPLICATES. With most types of possessions, one is more than enough.
- ▶ Learn to let go. (See page 171.)
- ▶ Avoid playing win-or-lose. (See page 173.)
- ▶ Set up ratios. For example, for every three pieces of clothing you keep, give up one.

MEASURE THE SPACE YOU HAVE. KEEP ONLY WHAT WILL FIT IN THAT SPACE.

▶ **DO:** Set time limits for sorting. This will help you stay on task.

▶ **DO:** Play games. Have a pile of shoes to tackle? For every shoe you can throw into a box from across the yard, you keep one pair of shoes.

▶ **DO:** Apply the rules regarding paperwork and files. (See page 53.)

▶ **DO:** Cull collections. Choose one or two things to honor.

▶ **DO:** Test for dust. Anything that has collected a coat of dust is not properly honored.

▶ **DO:** Get rid of "wish" clothes ("I wish I could still wear this").

▶ **DO:** Ditch dupes.

▶ **DO:** Take photos of large items you can't keep but will miss.

▶ **DO:** Downsize—can you compile paper files onto a disk?

▶ **DO:** Keep only a set number of DVDs, CDs, crafts projects, books, shoes, etc.

▶ **DO:** Update your technology (CDs versus albums; laptops versus large computers; small speakers versus towers, and so on).

▶ **DO:** Recycle unused gifts you don't like or need as gifts to someone else.

KEEP

TOSS

EACH HOUSE AVERAGES ABOUT ONE-HALF TON OF TRASH. THE *CLEAN SWEEP* GARBAGE TRUCK HAULS DEBRIS TO THE DUMP AFTER EVERY TWO EPISODES.

CLEAN *SWEEP* RECYCLES OLD NEWSPAPERS, MAGAZINES, SHREDDED PAPERWORK, PLASTIC, GLASS, AND ALUMINUM—SO CAN YOU!

PAPERWORK

WHAT TO KEEP AND HOW LONG TO KEEP IT

TAX RETURNS AND RECORDS
- Formal returns: Indefinitely
- Related documentation: 7 years

EXPENSES
- Receipts: 2 months if unrelated to taxes
- Utility bills: 1 year if unrelated to taxes

BANKING AND FINANCES
- Checks: Until they've been canceled
- Bank statements: 1 year
- Credit card statements: 6 months if unrelated to taxes
- Investments: Indefinitely

INCOME
- Pay stubs: 1 year

HOME
- Mortgage records: As long as you own the property, plus 4 years after selling it
- Improvements: 4 years after the sale of the property

HEALTH
- Medical records: 4 years, or indefinitely for chronic issues

INSURANCE
- Policies: As long as they are active
- Bills: As long as they are related to an active policy

CHAPTER 3

SELL
YOUR STUFF

Ahh, the weekend yard sale…On the best of days, the sun is shining, the birds are singing, you're making a profit off things you don't need or want, and someone is thrilled to score a deal on those same items. Talk about a win-win. Watch the weather reports and follow Tava's tips for success and you'll have a picture-perfect sale suitable for all audiences.

STEP 1 RESEARCH

If you don't frequent yard sales, spend a few hours one weekend checking them out. Look in the classifieds, keep an eye out for yard sale signs, and soak up what you see. Pay attention to which signs catch your eye. What wording piques your interest? What are the going rates for goods? What times and dates do others set? Sometimes stay-at-home moms and retirees are the most enthusiastic shoppers, and Fridays and/or Saturdays may work best for their schedules. Also find out what sale permits your local authorities require. Refrain from buying anything; if the clutter-collecting beast within can't be tamed, send a friend or family member in your place.

STEP 2 ADVERTISE

Put your ad in the classified section of your local newspaper to attract the biggest crowd. Mention specific popular items (furniture, antiques, electronics, CDs, toys, bikes, rugs, appliances, children's clothes) to draw serious shoppers. Papers usually require that you turn in information by noon the day before your sale date; some have package deals that run your ad from Thursday through Saturday. Place outdoor signs to lead traffic from nearby busy streets to your sale location. Place sale flyers on bulletin boards at the library and grocery, convenience shops, and self-service laundries.

SUPER SIGNS

A great yard sale sign:
▶ Catches the eye (neon color does the job).
▶ Is legible (even from a moving car).
▶ Mentions day, date, beginning and end times.
▶ Lists the sale address.
▶ Points the way with directive arrows (arrow-shape signs are great).
▶ Is posted in a logical spot (as seen from a car).

YARD SALE TOOL KIT

- ▶ Stickers or masking tape (for price tags)
- ▶ Permanent markers
- ▶ Discreet, safe money holder
- ▶ Cash ($30 in five-dollar bills, $20 in singles, $10 in quarters, $5 in dimes)
- ▶ Rope (for a temporary clothesline)
- ▶ An extension cord (for customers to plug in electronics)
- ▶ A mirror (to help customers decide on clothes and jewelry)
- ▶ Snacks and drinks (for sellers)
- ▶ Signs
- ▶ String or duct tape (to hang signs)
- ▶ Sunscreen
- ▶ Babysitter for kids and closed quarters for pets

STEP 3 SET UP

The best yard sales have room for the sale items, space for shoppers to browse, ample parking, and overhead protection in case of rain. Carports and garages are ideal venues, but if you don't have one, find the next best thing, or postpone your sale until the weather improves. After you pick your sale spot, set up tables or spread tarps or sheets on which to display items. Hang temporary clotheslines for clothing. Set up a comfortable place where you can sit if things get slow.

STEP 4 PREP AND DISPLAY

Do an honest review of your sale items and toss things that are not easily salvageable, such as stained, ripped, or dirty clothing and bedding. People often buy broken items and repair them on their own or use them to harvest parts, but there is a limit. Next, freshen up the sale items: Wipe down dust- or grime-covered merchandise; hang clothes or fold them neatly. Group like items together and arrange them in an inviting display. Place big-ticket items and electronics at the front of the sale to attract drive-by shoppers.

STEP 5 PRICE

Use your local research to set prices or check online auction houses for typical prices. Here are some options:

- ▶ Let buyers offer you their dream price and then bargain with them until you settle on a deal.
- ▶ Tag all items with specific prices, using stickers or marked-up masking tape.
- ▶ Charge the same price for all similar items: For example, books are 50 cents; CDs are $1; shoes are $3. Post signs to inform shoppers of these price categories.

Want to attract more shoppers to your yard sale? Take cues from this *Clean Sweep* event: Notice how the homeowners grouped like items—videos, furniture, books, etc.— and how they used folding tables to display goods. Also, they placed goods in plain sight for drive-by browsers and added inviting touches like balloons to attract attention. The result is a compact secondhand "store" that welcomes customers.

- Price by lot: for example, "Everything on this table: $1!"
- Color-code prices: for example, all pink stickers, $1; green stickers, $2; red stickers, 50 cents.

STEP 6 BARGAIN

The name of the game when it comes to yard sales is haggle, says Tava. So when a shopper offers you something less than your asking price, go back and forth a little on the price. No matter how much you come down, you still win: After all, they are paying you for your clutter…and hauling it away.

STEP 7 DONATE TO CHARITY

Whether you give a charitable thrift store the leftovers from your yard sale, forgo a sale altogether and donate every non-keeper, or contribute all yard sale proceeds to a favorite cause, the recipients always appreciate the generosity. Charity is a great way to overcome sentimental attachments too, because you know that the items will benefit people in need. As if that weren't motivation enough, many thrift stores pick up castoffs, and the estimated sale sum of all

continued on page 62

MAKE IT FUN!

BLOW UP BALLOONS: Put up balloons at the sale location and on yard sale signs advertising the event.

SERVE TREATS: Offer customers free (or low-priced) cupcakes, cookies, or candy.

AUCTION IT OFF: On the show, Tava sometimes sets up the sale as an auction. Appoint an auctioneer and let shoppers bid on items as they come up for sale. Try this when traffic is heavy and then revert to standard shopping when shopper numbers drop.

HIGHLIGHT A SECRET ITEM: Designate one item and when someone buys it, make a hubbub (toss confetti, cheer), and give the shopper a bonus item, like a "gift with purchase."

PLAY DRESS-UP: Look for costumes among the sale items and dress up accordingly. Past episodes of *Clean Sweep* have featured barbecue chefs and clowns.

"BY THE END OF A YARD SALE, WITHOUT FAIL, PEOPLE LEARN TO LET GO. IT'S AMAZING TO WATCH SOMETHING GO FROM BEING 'IMMENSELY IMPORTANT' TO BEING SOMETHING THEY GLEEFULLY SELL OR SEND OFF TO CHARITY. BY THE TIME THE DAY IS OVER, YOU'D BE HARD-PRESSED TO MAKE THEM TAKE IT BACK INTO THEIR HOUSE."

Tava is a pricing bandit with her permanent marker and stickers, two essentials for any yard sale. Researching prices online and at other neighborhood sales is worth your time, but Tava suggests taking a relaxed view of the bottom line. "Think of a price as a removal fee, one that a customer is paying you!" she says.

donated goods is tax-deductible. Call a week in advance to schedule a pickup; time it for the end of your yard sale or a day or two afterward. (You may get so inspired by your purged and redesigned rooms, you'll want a few more days to work on the rest of the house and find more goods to donate. *Clean Sweep* families often do!)

STEP 8 GET COMPETITIVE

On the show, a little healthy competition always spurs the salesperson within. At home, pit parents against kids, husband against wife, partner against partner, and so on. Let every person on each team choose an item from the toss or sell pile; the group who sells the most gets to keep their chosen items. Or, if everything must go, let the winners keep a percentage of the overall profit. Take the entire household out to dinner with the remaining cash or choose a house present that everyone agrees on.

WHAT DID YOU BUY AT A CLEAN SWEEP SALE?

"A camera. It was very cool, and I've always wanted to take up photography."

"A pair of chairs...they had great lines, and I re-covered them. Now they are in my bedroom."

"I've bought NOTHING, because Tava has me tied up inside the house so I can finish designing."

"An 1850s desk, a Russian jewelry box, a little drum, and a tiny bomber jacket for a friend's 2-year-old. Thanks to being on the show, I only buy things if it's something really useful to me or if it's something special and I have a place for it."

"I bought wooden pole karate swords. I got the brilliant idea that it'd be fun to use them to play with my oldest son. Ultimately it just became something for him to chase me around the house with. Needless to say, I don't bring stuff home anymore."

YARD SALE DO'S AND DON'TS

▶ **Do offer broken toys and electronics. (Some people enjoy tinkering.)**

   ▶ Don't be dishonest about the condition of damaged goods.

▶ **Do let customers test electronics. (Use an extension cord.)**

   ▶ Don't let strangers into your house.

   ▶ Do stash your money in a central location. (Try a hip bag.)

   ▶ Don't leave your money unattended.

   ▶ Do take cash or checks from people you know and trust. (Still ask for all pertinent info to track the buyer.)

   ▶ Don't take checks from strangers.

   ▶ Do have a partner at your sale. (Buddies are smart for safety reasons.)

   ▶ Don't forget to invite your neighbors to hold simultaneous sales. Multifamily yard sales draw bigger crowds.

▶ **Do be prepared for people to stop by earlier than your advertised time. (They're called "early birds.")**

   ▶ Don't be afraid to ask them to come back later, when you're open for business.

   ▶ Do plan your sale the night before. (The earlier the better.)

   ▶ Don't place sale items outside unattended.

   ▶ Do have a phone nearby in case of emergencies. (A cell phone should suffice.)

   ▶ Don't forget to take down your signs after the sale.

PART 3
MAKEOVER TIME

Chew on this: Every *Clean Sweep* episode yields one-half ton of trash. Yep, that's 1,000 pounds of clutter that's pulled out of each house, junk that once thoroughly choked the life out of its lodgings. Liken the purged house to someone who has just dropped an enormous amount of weight, and you're talking about a major change—but not quite a total one. To make the overhaul complete, the design team from *Clean Sweep* conducts a makeover, transforming a cluttered, sickly "before" into a truly amazing "after."

Devoted to the *Clean Sweep* code ("Form always follows function!"), Angelo, Molly, Kelli, and James are pros at making "after" rooms flawlessly functional yet ever so chic. "Peter and I talk about it all the time," says Angelo. "You can't have one without the other!" So whether you're into cool, mod looks, soothing spalike spaces, or playful places that pop with color, keep reading to find finished looks that pair high function with high fashion.

CHAPTER 4

FUNCTION
RULES

In designing your new room, function comes first. (Color, mood, and decor come later; a truly organized room plan always puts the horse before the cart.) Since you've already purged and sorted your belongings, only vital keeper items remain, which means you can finally tweak the plans you dreamed up in earlier stages. Before you tackle the next steps, take a deep breath and solemnly repeat the *Clean Sweep* oath: Form must follow function!

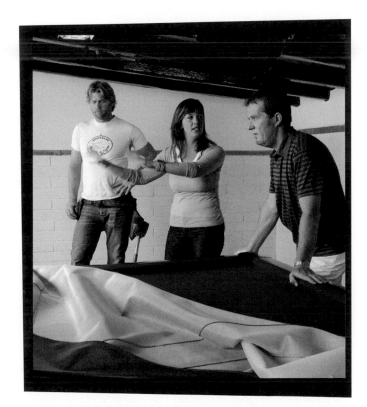

STEP 1 REASSESS THE ROOM

"Your first ideas are not always your best ideas," says James, referring to your original assessment of your cluttered space. "So edit yourself. Remember that first and foremost, you always have to determine how you want the space to function. Take a look around the empty room and make sure your initial zones—the activity areas a space needs to harbor—still ring true. Ask yourself again, 'What do I need from this space?'"

STEP 2 MEASURE REALITY

While you're looking at the room, take stock of what Kelli calls the room's overall bone structure. "Focus on the shape of the room," says Kelli, "the angles of the ceiling, the location of doors and windows, and built-in units and closets." Pay attention to the details and note the room's shortcomings and strengths. You'll want to play up the good (views, cool architectural elements, built-in storage) and cover up or compensate for the weaknesses (poor lighting, cramped quarters, no built-ins). Measure the outer edge of the room—where the floor meets the walls—so you can sketch a precise floor plan. Clutter often piles up because people think they have more space than they actually do, says Peter; this mapping exercise forces clutterbugs to accept reality.

STEP 3 JUMP ONTO THE GRID

Now that you've got your space measured, make copies of page 188. Each square on the grid equals 1 square foot in the actual room. Transfer the wall measurements onto the grid to create a floor plan; include architectural features such as doors, windows, fireplaces, closets, and stairs. Next, add your activity zones. "Make a bubble diagram," advises James. "Draw one bubble to contain each zone and place it in its logical space." For example, if you have a studio space, you'll have a living area, a kitchen, a dining area, and a sleeping area. The kitchen bubble will encircle the built-in appliances and the bed will likely be far from the front door. If you have an L-shape room and it needs to contain two activity zones, use one leg of the L for each zone.

STEP 4 PLAN TO STASH YOUR STUFF

In chapter 2, you guesstimated what furniture you'd keep and what organizational systems (closets, shelves, and so on) you would need to add. Now that you know what's actually returning to the room, reexamine the belongings you have versus the existing storage. Kelli recalls a couple who had almost 700 DVDs in their home: "It was like a video store, and movies were obviously an important passion of theirs," she says. "They ended up cutting the collection down to 500, but I still had to figure out what organizational systems would answer the need." Take a look at what you'll restock the space with, and assign a place for every item.

STEP 5 ARRANGE YOUR FURNITURE

On pages 184–187, you'll find sample furniture shapes. Make a copy of those pages and measure your keeper furniture pieces. Cut out the corresponding furniture shapes and arrange them on your room grid. (Note: one grid square equals 1 square foot). Place items in appropriate zones. For example, put an entertainment hutch near the cable wire outlets and give a sofa a view of the TV. This is a puzzle game designers play, one that lets them arrange a room without having to drag furniture around.

STEP 6 FILL IN THE HOLES

Now that you've got the furniture in place on the floor plan, take a look at what's missing. Need a nightstand by the bed? Need something to store books and magazines? Do what the designers do and shop the rest of your house for underutilized pieces that might answer your needs. If you don't have anything on hand, buy or build pieces to fit the measurements of your space. Make to-scale furniture shapes for these new pieces and affix them to your floor plan with repositionable adhesive tape.

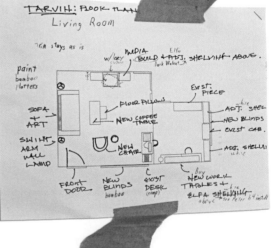

70

Shelf System
TOOL KIT

- ▶ Ready-to-assemble wire shelf system*
- ▶ Pencil
- ▶ Tape measure
- ▶ Closet grid plan
- ▶ Level
- ▶ Hammer
- ▶ Stud finder
- ▶ Screwdriver
- ▶ Drill and bits

* *Clean Sweep* organizes most closets with boxed wire shelf sets. These come with simple instructions that are novice-friendly.

Depending on the size of the project, give yourself 4 to 6 hours to set up and restock your shelves. Find the shelf sets at organization stores, home improvement centers, or online.

Shelf
PLANNING

You can use the grid on page 188 to map out the perfect closet. Measure the height and width of the space and draw that frontal view onto the grid. Consider the items you're going to put back in the closet and sketch the ideal configuration of shelves, bars, and hooks for your belongings. Include a chest of drawers or filing cabinets as needed. Also use the grid to map other shelf configurations, such as wall-mounted shelves over a desk, workbench, or craft station.

PLAN THE PERFECT CLOSET

To establish a functional room that you can keep organized, you need excellent closet and shelf systems. Make sure everything going back into the closet needs to be there—if it doesn't, find a new spot for it. Then catalog the existing closet space and ask yourself:

- ▶ Will the current shelf formation serve your needs?
- ▶ Is the full height of the closet utilized?
- ▶ Are there single or stacked bars for hanging clothes?

▶ Do you need more shelves, drawers, sliding wire baskets, or hanging space?

- ▶ Do you need shoe storage, tie and belt hooks, or shelves to store office supplies and equipment?
- ▶ What didn't work before?

Make another copy of the grid on page 188, this time to sketch a front view of your closet. Measure the outline of the closet, pencil it onto the grid, and draw the ideal setup for your belongings. Design an arrangement that will give you easy access to the items you use most often.

BACKGROUND: The owners of this space amassed so many collectibles that they hadn't seen the floor of their living room for six years. And eating in the adjoining dining nook? Forget it. Post-purge, James gave the couple a traditional English-style den and cozy cafe alcove with subtle storage solutions to showcase the best of their keepsakes.

PROBLEM: Sure, the space was loaded with cool valuables—imported masks, vintage lampshades, antique furniture—but the couple had neither room nor use for much of the loot.

SOLUTION: Assigning every keeper to its own place in the room (on a shelf, a wall, a hook, and so on) restored order and honored each item properly.

PROBLEM: Frog puppets and storytelling gear were lumped with Granny's hand-me-downs; the space lacked general purpose, flow, and a cohesive vision.

SOLUTION: Items were pared down to those that related to the purposes of the two rooms, and an overall color scheme unified the spaces.

PROBLEM: When a space becomes a dumping ground, it's got zero utility. To traverse this living room, the couple had to climb from pile to pile.

SOLUTION: A serious purge afforded James room to move, and he quickly established zones such as this reading nook, *left*, where the homeowners can sit and enjoy a good book; an ample seating area offers room for guests too. To tie the living and dining areas together visually, James matched fabrics, outfitting a vintage chair in a slipcover that echoes the sage green pillows on the banquette.

PROBLEM: For all the furniture they had amassed, the couple didn't own a table large enough to accommodate guests.

SOLUTION: Eric built a custom table topper to rest on the existing occasional table, transforming it from decorative to functional. Now there's seating room for four.

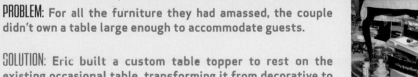

PROBLEM: Fireplace—what fireplace? Even if you could spot it in the room's once-cluttered condition, lighting a fire there would have been unthinkable.

SOLUTION: Getting rid of the piles uncovered the fireplace as a focal point. The mantel became a showcase for collectibles that made the keeper cut. The mirror provides a nice contrast to the dark walls.

PROBLEM: With all the stuff stacked everywhere, there was no centralized place for paying bills and no space for the couple to manage their self-run businesses.

SOLUTION: A keeper vintage desk became an all-purpose workstation. Basic wall-mounted shelving stocked with stylish file boxes upped the work zone's storage capacity.

LOVE SEAT WITH BUILT-IN BOOKSHELF

TOOLS NEEDED

- ▶ Tape measure
- ▶ Table saw
- ▶ Safety goggles
- ▶ Finish nailer
- ▶ Stir sticks
- ▶ Paint tray
- ▶ Paintbrushes

MATERIALS NEEDED

- ▶ Two 4×8-foot sheets 1-inch MDF (medium-density fiberboard)
- ▶ One 17×54-inch piece of luaun for the backing
- ▶ 2-inch nails
- ▶ Wood glue
- ▶ Primer
- ▶ Latex paint, dark brown or desired color

STEP 1

Determine the size of your finished love seat/bench. **Note:** The bench *opposite* is 54 inches long, 17 inches tall, and 24 inches wide. The underside of the bench has four cubbies, each 7×25½ inches (see A).

STEP 2

Cut two pieces of MDF 24×54 inches (for the top and bottom), three pieces 15×24 inches (for the sides and divider), and two pieces 24×25½ inches (for the shelves). Glue and then nail the 15×24-inch sides to the 24×54-inch bottom piece (see B). Center the 15×24-inch divider on the bottom; glue and then nail it in place. Turn the unit onto one side; glue and then nail one of the 24×25½-inch shelf pieces to one side piece and the divider, centering the shelf piece. Repeat with the remaining shelf piece. Glue and then nail the top to the sides and divider (see C and D). Glue and then nail the luaun back in place.

STEP 3

Prime the entire bench; let dry. Paint the entire bench; let dry. (To save time, the *Clean Sweep* crew primes the boards before assembling the piece.)

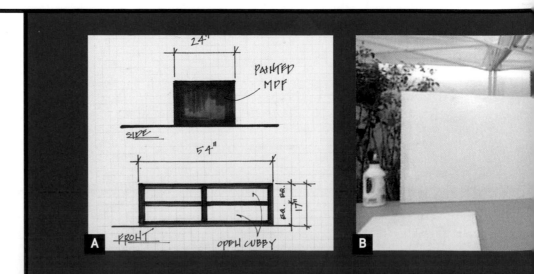

C

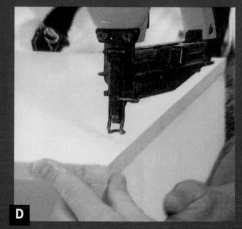

D

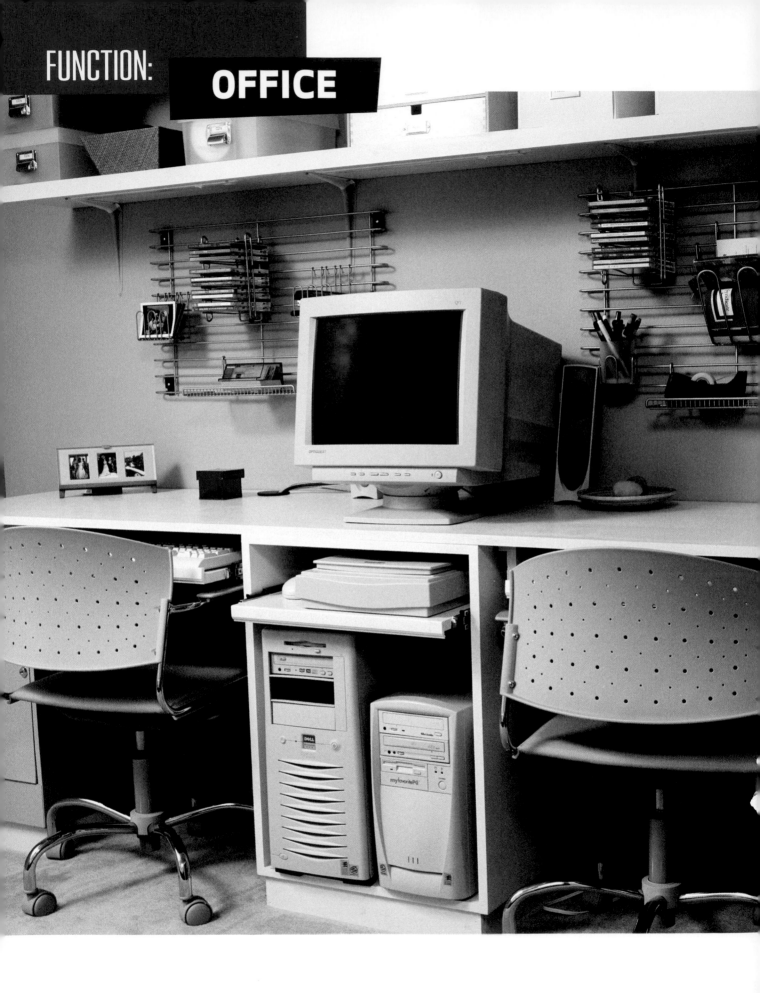

BACKGROUND: This room housed a couple's three C's—their computers, their crafts, and their company. That's a tall order for such a small space, especially when it's one that is filled to the brim with clutter. After the family weathered a thorough sorting process, the resulting space became a testimony to the beauty of function-driven zones, mood-setting color, and efficient organization. Compliments of Kelli, it boasts a new sofa bed and one hardworking desk.

PROBLEM: A plague of piles left only a few bare inches of space on the desk top, so working was almost impossible.

SOLUTION: Eric made a new desk with room for two and added storage space as well: filing cabinets, a wall-mounted shelf, and wire wall racks freed up space on the desk top.

PROBLEM: The wife had a cherished sewing machine, but there was nowhere to use it in this storage unit of a room.

SOLUTION: Clearing the excess from the desk top created a versatile work space where she can sew to her heart's content.

PROBLEM: Even office equipment was piled high, creating a precarious mess and risking damage to sensitive electronics. The sprawling work area was completely inefficient.

SOLUTION: Sliding platforms were built for the keyboards and scanner; a module houses two computer towers belowdeck; the nearby closet has been reworked to accommodate overflow, such as the seldom-used printer. Everything in the redesigned space has a specific storage place within sensible reach of the desk.

PROBLEM: Grandmother often came to care for the couple's young son, but she had to clear off a cotlike bed surrounded by a sea of junk to sleep. The clutter kept the room from feeling like a welcoming guest space.

SOLUTION: The design team added a comfortable seating piece that converts into a bed, so the room now functions more clearly as guest quarters.

PROBLEM: Towering boxes rendered the closet dysfunctional. The owners couldn't even shut the doors.

SOLUTION: Patient sorting through the contents of each box reduced the load to carefully chosen keepers stored in fashionable, practical new containers. A reworked shelf system accommodates seldom-used equipment, supplies, and reference material. Chalkboard paint on the sliding doors adds a fun touch of functionality.

"COLOR IS SO IMPORTANT FOR SETTING MOODS. PALE BLUES, FOR INSTANCE, ARE VERY CALMING."

DESK FOR TWO

HOW-TO

TOOLS NEEDED

- ▶ Tape measure
- ▶ Table saw
- ▶ Safety goggles
- ▶ Wood glue
- ▶ Electric screwdriver
- ▶ Finish nailer
- ▶ Stir sticks
- ▶ Paint tray
- ▶ Paintbrushes

MATERIALS NEEDED

- ▶ 4×8-foot sheets ³⁄₄-inch MDF (medium-density fiberboard)
- ▶ 2-inch nails
- ▶ 6 drawer slides (track and slide portions) and mounting hardware
- ▶ Primer
- ▶ Latex paint, white or other desired color
- ▶ Two 2-drawer filing cabinets

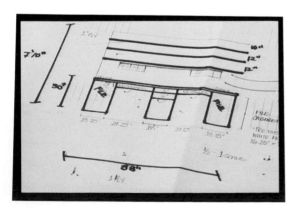

STEP 1

Measure the dimensions of your filing cabinets; the depth will determine the depth of the desk. Decide how long you want the desk top to be. **Note:** The desk shown *above* is 8 feet, 8 inches (104 inches) long, 30 inches tall, and 24 inches deep. The desk top rests on the filing cabinets; to raise the top to a comfortable working height, the filing cabinets and center unit stand on 3-inch-tall bases. Each kneehole is 27¼ inches wide; the center unit (18 inches wide) has a pullout shelf for a scanner or printer.

STEP 2

For the desk top, cut one piece of MDF to the size determined in Step 1. For a 30-inch-tall desk, cut two pieces of MDF 29¼ inches by the depth determined in Step 1; these pieces will be the sides of the desk. With the desk top right side down, glue and then nail the sides to the underside of the desk top at each short end.

STEP 3

For the center computer storage unit, cut two pieces of MDF 26¼ inches by the depth determined in Step 1. These will be the sides. Cut two pieces of MDF 18 inches wide by the depth of the desk; these will be the top and bottom of the unit. Glue and then nail the sides to the top and bottom pieces (see A, B, and E). For the scanner shelf, cut one piece of MDF 18 inches minus the depth of the drawer slides. Make the shelf the depth of the desk top. Attach the slide portion of two drawer slides to the sides of the scanner shelf (see A, B, C, and D). Attach two drawer tracks inside the computer storage unit, 12 inches from the top (see F and G). Center the unit on the underside of the desk top; glue and then nail it in place (see H).

STEP 4

For keyboard shelf supports, cut two pieces of MDF 5 inches by the depth of the desk top. Measure 16½ inches (or the width of your filing cabinet) from the inside edge of each side and glue and then nail a 5-inch-wide piece to the underside of the desk top, parallel to the side. Attach a drawer track for the keyboard shelf to each 5-inch-wide piece, aligning it with the bottom edge. Attach a matching drawer track to each outer side of the computer storage unit, 5 inches from the top. Turn the desk right side up.

STEP 5

Cut two pieces of MDF 26½ inches by the depth of the desk top; these will be the keyboard shelves. Attach the slide portion of the drawer slides to the sides of the shelves.

STEP 6

For each of the three bases, cut two pieces of MDF 3 inches wide by 15 inches long and two pieces 3 inches by the depth of the desk minus 2 inches. Glue and nail the pieces together to make a box. Prime and then paint all pieces. Let dry.

STEP 7

Stand the filing cabinets on their bases. Position the desk over the filing cabinets. Slide the keyboard shelves into the desk openings.

CHAPTER 5

DESIGN DICTATES

Angelo calls this stage—the decorating phase—dress-up time. But what if you're at a loss as to what your room should wear? Put your trepidation aside and let the *Clean Sweep* design team walk you through the following makeover master plan to add flair to your function.

Opposite and above: Basement rooms like this one tend to lack natural light. Rather than blast the space with cold, glaring overheads, opt for something softer and you'll get a cozier feeling overall. Here Kelli used a combination of light-colored (and therefore light-reflecting) paint, natural stained wood timber ceilings, and an ambient hanging lamp to create a mellow mood.

STEP 1 GET MOODY

Previous chapters taught you how to address function and map out a floor plan. Now it's time to move from intellect to emotion: How does the room make you feel? The more you connect with a space, the better you feel in it, the more you'll use it, and the more you'll want to maintain its organized appearance. People connect with rooms that have good flow; flow is the harmony that comes from careful layout, color, and lighting choices. If these pieces of the puzzle are out of whack, there is disharmony or discomfort. Gauging your feelings about the room will help you understand what's working or what needs to be adjusted.

STEP 2 FINE-TUNE FURNITURE PLACEMENT

By now your furniture is positioned in logical zones, but as you look around your room with design in mind, ask yourself if you've taken the pieces hostage. "People tend to put their furniture up against walls like it's in some firing squad lineup," says Angelo. "Instead push furniture away from the walls if you have the room, even just a little bit. That alone opens a space, makes it airy, and creates walkways. Don't be afraid to put things—like sofas—on a diagonal. Remember, you're not setting anything in stone; you're just moving furniture around, and you won't know what feels right until you play a little." As you look at the layout, you'll know you have found a winning combination if it feels good, makes sense, and allows you to move freely.

STEP 3 HYPE THE GOOD AND HIDE THE BAD

They say it's the little things that make every person an individual. The same is true with houses and rooms—the details make the difference. Take in the little things, the pros and cons of the area you're making over, regarding the space from the perspective of design and emotion. "Does the light change throughout the day?" asks Molly. If so, is there something that you want to place in those sunlit pools, a painting or a cherished vase you want to highlight? Do you want to minimize window treatments to take advantage of the light? Or are there problem spots—ugly ducts, outdated ceiling fans, or a "cottage cheese" ceiling—that need concealing or updating? Perhaps it's time to build a screen or sew a curtain to cover up the flaws.

PICK A KEEPER COLOR

Are you having a tough time settling on a color? Here are some ideas:

TAKE THE LOVE TEST: James shows a color wheel to *Clean Sweep* families and asks them to pick out three favorite colors and three least favorite ones too. "That way," he says, "I have the full spectrum and know the boundaries of where to go and where not to go." Do this yourself with paint chips from a paint or home improvement store.

CHOOSE DECAF OR FULLY LOADED: Kelli says moods should lead the way: If you want to feel serene (as in a bedroom), go for muted shades, and if you want to be energized (say, in an office), go for brights.

PLAY COPYCAT: Flip through magazines and pull out the ads and room photos that look the best to you. Mimic their use and choice of color.

LET YOUR KEEPERS LEAD YOU: If you decide Grandma's portrait is important, offers Kelli, pull some colors from the painting and use them throughout the room. Or if you've decided a rug must stay, play up some of its colors elsewhere.

CONTRAST TO COMPLEMENT: If you have a dark piece of furniture that's a keeper, place it against a lighter-color wall to showcase the piece.

COLOR IT THRICE: Use a trio of colors—a main overall color, a secondary color as an accent (for the inside of built-in shelves, panels of walls or doors, or below wainscoting), and a third color for the trim.

STEP 4 COLOR WITH COURAGE

Color tends to scare people, says Angelo. "And that's a shame, because it's one of the least expensive ways to give a room a massive overhaul and a new look. Plus, a fresh coat of paint—no matter the color—always inspires you to keep a place looking neat." Maybe you fear making the "wrong" color choice. If so, know that color is a personal preference; sometimes experimenting is the only way to get to know yourself and your favorite shades. It's easy to cover any missteps, so why hesitate? To determine your favorite color, Angelo recommends that you think about your favorite houses, hotels, restaurants, and shops. What color palettes do these dream spaces wear—earth tones, rich jewel tones, eye-popping brights, or muted neutrals? A little mental research will lead you to the best selection for you. Try a patch test, and consult chapter 6 for painting advice.

Vibrant yellow walls up this room's energy level and show off existing features such as the brushed metal wall sconce and a row of blue pendent lamps. Pairing a mod magenta sofa with a cool glass coffee table, unfussy floating shelves, and sculptural table lanterns rounds out the contemporary look. White accessories make a visual bridge between bold magenta and warm gold, lightening and brightening the scheme.

STEP 5 MAKE SUPERFICIAL CHANGES

Once you've stocked your room with the most functionally fit furniture, ask yourself point-blank: Does everything look good? In one episode, Kelli encountered a tiny bedroom with a terrific chest of drawers and an entertainment center. The pieces were unequal in height, and the exposed TV was unsightly in the otherwise serene space. The solution? Eric leveled the two by building a new base for the shorter piece; then he fashioned a countertop to cap the unit as a whole. Kelli added a grass window shade to conceal the shelved TV. The result was a recycled, fully functional, attractive storage system. Slipcovers, fresh paint, and new hardware are other options for the budget-conscious makeover.

STEP 6 ACCESSORIZE

To make a space flow without adding clutter, go vertical, says Kelli. In other words, take to the walls with artwork. All the show's designers agree that reformed clutterbugs stay clutter-free when surface areas (such as coffee tables, side tables, dressers, nightstands, and countertops) are minimally accessorized and when floors host no piles or "collections" (clutter masquerading as keepsakes). Like any functional piece, every decoration ought to serve a purpose. Does it add a splash of color that works with your overall scheme? Is it dear to you? If it doesn't pass muster, put the item out of sight, out of the room, or out of the house.

MONEY MATTERS

What's Your STYLE?

"My first couple," says Molly, "was a little on the punk side—she had hot pink hair and a shirt that read 'Fabulous Disaster.' Someone asked me what on earth made me think I could paint a room in their house bright orange and pink. I said, 'Umm…did you see them? They were broadcasting their style!' The funny thing was they knew their taste in fashion, but their home wasn't announcing it; the place was pretty conservative."

Style SUGGESTION:

"Look around at your favorite things to find your personal style," offers Molly. Find repetition in colors, patterns, textures, objects. Are you into organic shapes or geometric ones? Let what you love guide your design choices.

"As for my style?" Molly says, "I'd say it's pretty funny. I've got a lawn deer on my dining room table!"

Limiting how much you'll invest in your room makeover doesn't mean you'll be shortchanged on your results. Setting limits in your financial world is as important as limiting the amount of stuff in your home; limits are part of any well-organized life. Before you buy a single can of paint, establish a decorating budget, including money for storage bins and organizational systems. Then consider these money-saving style secrets from the *Clean Sweep* designers.

▶ Dress up inexpensive store-bought curtains by adding ribbon trim and details with a hot-glue gun.

▶ Make custom sconces by gluing shells or other heat-safe materials to store-bought metal sconces.

▶ Frame a piece of favorite fabric, wallpaper, or wrapping paper for low-cost custom artwork.

▶ Use synthetic silks instead of true silk.

▶ Substitute burlap for linen.

▶ Hang woven grass shades instead of bamboo matchstick shades.

▶ Use polyester pillow inserts instead of feather ones.

▶ Add ribbon accents instead of tassels on pillows and bedding.

BACKGROUND: Two teenage brothers shared this spacious, loftlike room. Besides the sleeping area, it harbored a study zone and an entertainment hub where the boys watched TV and movies and played video games. After a serious purge of junk and funk, Angelo worked his magic to make the room a cool blend of form and function.

PROBLEM: A big water bed frame housed a tiny spring mattress; the eyesore combo discouraged pride of ownership and offered no motivation to make the bed.

SOLUTION: Angelo installed identical beds and bedding, so the sleeping zone is stylistically in sync. Now the brothers make their beds in an instant by simply spreading the comforters over the sheets.

PROBLEM: The old nightstands didn't suit the color, style, and proportions of the beds. The stained walls needed help.

SOLUTION: Painting the sleeping area a soothing shade of blue gave the space a cozy feel conducive to snoozing. The brothers scored new blue nightstands that complement the fresh color palette. Angelo placed the two bedside units against each other for a unified look.

PROBLEM: The window covering was nothing more than a plain bedsheet. Plus there was no separation of one brother's turf from the other's.

SOLUTION: Simple curtains on an inexpensive rod dressed up the window and repeated the bedding pattern. Orbs hung from the ceiling establish a boundary between two territories—a subtle but effective detail in such tight sleeping quarters.

PROBLEM: Desks covered in junk stifled good study habits. Bare, impersonal walls were a downer.

SOLUTION: Wall-mounted magazine racks organize paperwork and college brochures for easy reference. A door-hung cap rack keeps hats in order. The snowboard adds a splash of color to the walls, and the Bob Marley sketch contributes personality, celebrating the guys' musical tastes.

PROBLEM: Dirty, smelly clothes were scattered everywhere, and clothing storage was inadequate.

SOLUTION: Each teen got his own dirty clothes hamper and a newly built storage unit for clean clothes at the foot of his bed. Two new wardrobes offer space for overflow items.

"THE CHALLENGE WAS TO CREATE A SPACE COOL ENOUGH THAT THEY WERE EXCITED ABOUT KEEPING IT ORGANIZED."

PROBLEM: The long room had no visual boundaries for zones. Randomly placed furniture such as the footlockers encouraged haphazard storage of miscellaneous junk.

SOLUTION: By painting the entertainment and study areas a contrasting yet harmonious color, Angelo set this end of the room apart from the sleeping half. He assigned the footlockers to serve as coffee tables in the media corner, and used them to handily store games, tapes, and electronics.

PROBLEM: Without the right color scheme, cool architectural details went unnoticed. The piles of stuff all over the room detracted attention from display-worthy items.

SOLUTION: Painting walls blue and wall nooks a contrasting pale green showcased a prized trophy collection. A storage ottoman keeps surface clutter to a minimum.

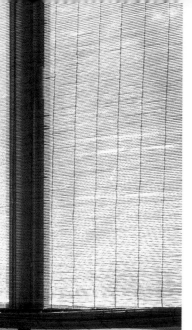

BACKGROUND: This den started off as a dumping ground disaster where huge piles of toys mingled with the proud papa's musical instruments and Mom's once-cherished paintings. A pair of spike-ended tiki torches casually stored there posed a potential safety problem too. Once the parents had pared down the toys to three bins and sorted through their own clutter, James designed a zone-perfect place with half of the space for adults and half for kids. Created around the surfer-dude husband's favorite Hawaiian theme, the result reduced him to tears.

PROBLEM: The room was unsafe for the kids as there were sharp, breakable objects within easy reach.

SOLUTION: The fenced-in area for the kids created a giant playpen, with room at the other end for Mom and Dad (or babysitters) to keep an eye on them. Safety features such as a lock and hinges on the adult side of the gate keep little fingers away from possible danger zones.

PROBLEM: The room suffered from a bad case of the catchalls and had no overall vision, designated activity zones, or flow.

SOLUTION: James created two zones for the room's purposes—playroom and adult lounge—and separated them with a kid-safe fence bolted into the floor for sturdiness. Now function entered the picture and the space became a hot spot in the house.

PROBLEM: With its boring color scheme, the old den lacked energy—it didn't inspire the kids to play, and it didn't encourage their parents to relax here either.

SOLUTION: By painting the room mango, blue, and a shade of sand, the whole space acquired a cheerily mellow beach feel that worked with the bright palette of the kids' playhouse and toys and the tropical look of the dad's tiki torches and bamboo furniture.

PROBLEM: The space lacked storage and thus the toddlers' toys were tossed everywhere in the room. Mom dreamed of a room where the kids' creativity could reign.

SOLUTION: James designed a wall of storage with shelves for the toys, hanging space for dress-up clothes, bins for easy-reach games, and built-in chalkboard and drawing stations.

BACKGROUND: Children's playroom or parental storage unit? You make the call. Clothes, old gifts, photo albums, and stacks of other stuff made it impossible for the kids to find their toys, let alone play safely in this space. After the purge, Angelo brought in all new furniture and storage pieces to create a junior computer station, a dress-up corner, and a general activity area that's perfect for games, movie watching, and sleepovers.

PROBLEM: The old desk was designed for grown-ups, not for the small kids who actually used it. Huge bin drawers encouraged the stashing of junk instead of necessities.

SOLUTION: Pairing a coffee table and a seat cushion chair, Angelo created a kid-friendly desk that makes computer work less intimidating and more like play. Plastic bins and photo boxes replaced the wire drawers to create tidy order.

PROBLEM: Even the homeowners' friends used the space to store their overflow clutter. The lack of space for activities put family game time on the back burner.

SOLUTION: Designating the room as a family play space meant everything unrelated to play had to go. Post-purge, the family stocked shelves and tables with keepers such as games, costumes, and toys.

PROBLEM: The kids scattered their dress-up props amid the clutter so the clothes were always hard to find and rumpled.

SOLUTION: A kid-scale wardrobe provided a central storage place for costumes. Throughout the room, toys were placed on easy-to-reach shelves, giving the children responsibility for putting away their own things.

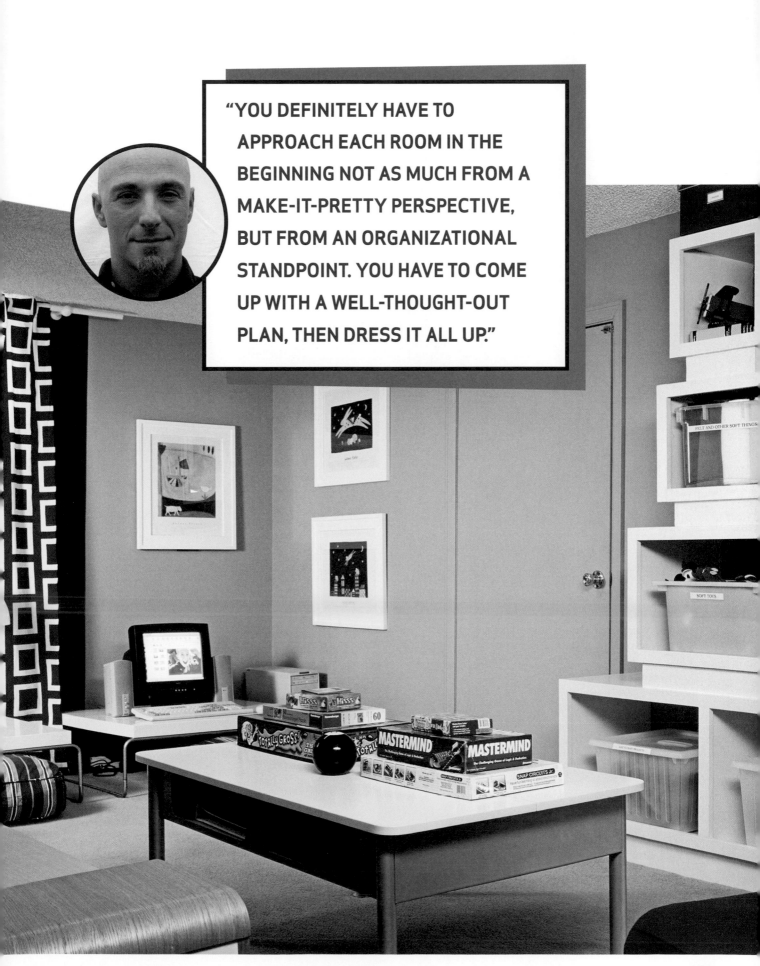

"YOU DEFINITELY HAVE TO APPROACH EACH ROOM IN THE BEGINNING NOT AS MUCH FROM A MAKE-IT-PRETTY PERSPECTIVE, BUT FROM AN ORGANIZATIONAL STANDPOINT. YOU HAVE TO COME UP WITH A WELL-THOUGHT-OUT PLAN, THEN DRESS IT ALL UP."

PROBLEM: Forget barreling down the stairs and into the playroom—hide-and-seek was the only game possible in the chaotic space.

SOLUTION: Creating a clear path for entering the room was essential. Introducing a sensible furniture layout made the space safe and usable for kids.

UP AND DOWN

Anytime you can use a piece of furniture for more than one purpose, you're maximizing the functionality of the room. *Clean Sweep* designers are pros at tracking down multifunctional pieces, such as the main coffee table and sofa in this room. If you can find such versatile pieces, consider selling older furniture that doesn't work as hard, and use the proceeds to finance new items.

The tabletop lifts to reveal hidden storage and acts as a TV tray for anyone sitting on the sofa. The easy-wipe table surface is ideal for kids.

Shift the pillows around to convert the sofa into a bed that's equally comfortable for adult guests, kids on sleepovers, or quick impromptu naps for those of any age.

TOOLS NEEDED

- ▶ Tape measure
- ▶ Table saw
- ▶ Safety goggles
- ▶ Finish nailer
- ▶ Stir sticks
- ▶ Paint tray
- ▶ Paintbrushes

MATERIALS NEEDED

- ▶ 4×8-foot sheets ¾-inch MDF (medium density fiberboard)
- ▶ 2-inch nails
- ▶ Wood glue
- ▶ 1×2-inch furring strips for facings
- ▶ Primer
- ▶ Latex paint, white and gray or desired colors

Note: The shelving unit *opposite* has four stacked shelves: 18×48 inches, 16×24 inches, 14×18 inches, and 14×14 inches. Each shelf is 14 inches deep and is supported by a 3-inch-tall base. The bottom unit has a middle divider; the other three shelves do not.

STEP 1

For the 18×48-inch unit, cut one piece of MDF 18×48 inches (for the back), two pieces 14×48 inches (for the top and bottom), and three pieces 14×16½ inches (for the sides and divider). Center the divider on the underside or wrong side of the top piece; then glue and nail it in place (see A and B). Glue and then nail the sides to the top. Flip the unit over and glue and then nail the bottom to the sides and divider. Glue and then nail the 18×48-inch back to the unit.

STEP 2

From the 1×2-inch furring strips cut two 18-inch-long strips for the sides, two 44-inch-long strips for the top and bottom edges, and one 14-inch strip for the divider. These will face the front edges of the unit. Glue and then nail the strips to the edges of the MDF so the 1-inch edge of the strip is flush with the outside surface of the unit.

STEP 3

For the base, cut two pieces of MDF 3×44 inches and two pieces 3×13¾ inches. Glue and then nail these pieces together to form a frame on which the 18×48-inch unit will stand. Center the frame on the bottom of the unit so the unit overhangs the length of the frame by 2 inches on each side. Glue and then nail the frame to the bottom of the unit.

Repeat this procedure to make the remaining units, cutting pieces as follows:

For the 16×24-inch unit, cut one piece of MDF 16×24 inches (for the back), two pieces 14×24 inches (for the top and bottom), and two pieces 14×14½ inches (for the sides). For facings, from 1×2 furring strips cut two 16-inch pieces and two 20-inch pieces. For the base, cut two pieces of MDF 3×20 inches and two pieces 3×13¾ inches.

For the 14×18-inch unit, cut three pieces of MDF 14×18 inches (for the back, top, and bottom) and two pieces 14×12½ inches (for the sides). For facings, from 1×2 furring strips cut four 14-inch strips. For the base, cut two pieces of MDF 3×14 inches and two pieces 3×13¾ inches.

For the 14×14-inch unit, cut three pieces of MDF 14×14 inches (for the back, top, and bottom) and two pieces 12½×14 inches (for the sides). For the facings, from 1×2 furring strips cut two 14-inch strips and two 10-inch strips. For the base, cut two pieces of MDF 3×10 inches and two pieces 3×13¾ inches.

STEP 4

Center the completed 16×24-inch unit on top of the 18×48-inch unit; glue and then nail to secure (see C). Repeat to attach remaining units.

STEP 5

Prime the entire shelving unit; let dry. Paint the interior of each shelf gray; let dry. Paint the facings and the exterior of each shelf white; let dry.

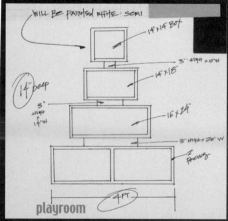

CHAPTER 6

PAINT IT PERFECT!

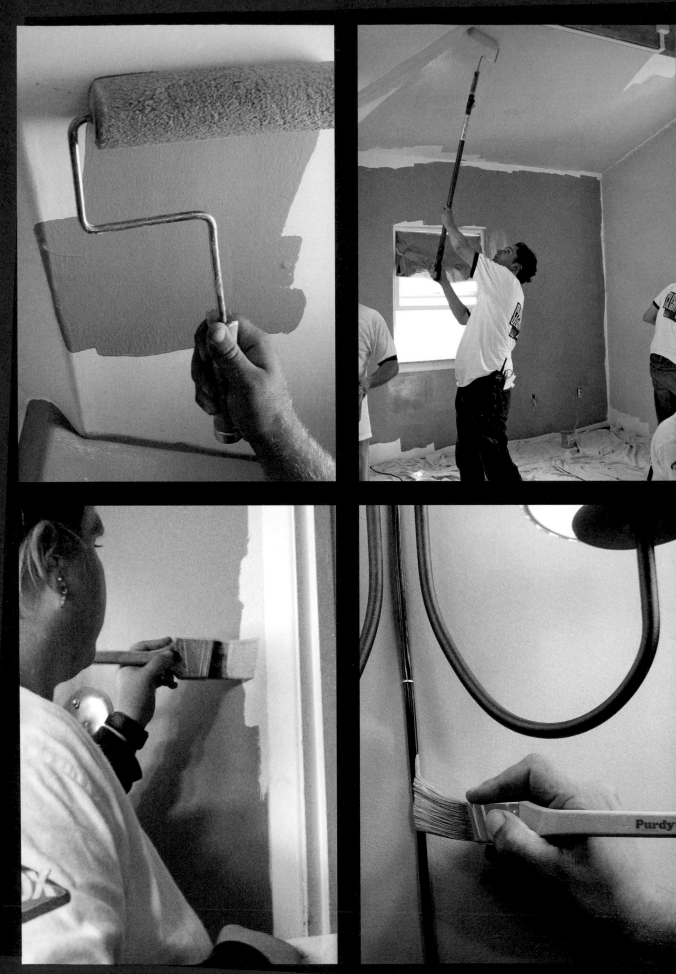

Give a formerly dysfunctional room a quickie color change, and suddenly the place becomes a blank slate. "With just a few hours and $30 to $60, you can get a tremendous transformation," says Angelo. "A new paint job is one of the easiest ways to jump into your organization makeover." He's got a point: Stand in a freshly painted empty space—crisp, clean, and colorful—and you're bound to be inspired by the possibilities. But how does the *Clean Sweep* crew do it so fast and so well? Here are their timesaving tricks.

STEP 1 PICK YOUR PAINT

After you choose your color (see page 88), it's time to buy the paint. Use this formula to determine how much you will need: Measure the length of each wall in feet and add the figures. Multiply the total by the wall height. Subtract about 15 to 20 feet for each window and standard-size door (or subtract exact measurements if you're a perfectionist). Divide the result by 300 (the average number of feet one paint gallon covers). The answer will tell you how many gallons (the full numbers) and quarts (the fractional numbers) to buy per coat. The *Clean Sweep* pros use flat latex paint because it dries the fastest and best conceals flaws (cracks, bumps, indentations) that spackling doesn't solve. However, if walls need to be washable, an eggshell finish is advisable—its slight sheen is easier to clean.

STEP 2 PREP THE SPACE

Invest a little sweat equity in cleaning and you'll have a beautifully bare canvas to paint. First empty the space as much as possible; use drop cloths to cover hard-to-move items such as pianos and case goods. Next, wipe the walls with a rag dampened in lukewarm soapy water. (Remove mildew stains with bleach-base products and ask for an anti-mildew additive in your new paint.) Thoroughly scrub all windowsills, door jambs, and shuttered doors before painting; otherwise dust bunnies will mar your paint job. Remove light switch, electrical outlet, and light fixture plates and cover exposed wiring with masking tape. (You can tape light switches in the "on" position.) Next, use surfacing compound to fill in holes, cracks, pockmarks, and other surface irregularities. When the compound dries, sand those patches smooth; also sand any rough or bumpy spots elsewhere. Cover the floor with drop cloths.

PAINT TOOL KIT

- Paint
- Drop cloths (made of an old sheet, plastic, or painter's canvas)
- Rollers (frames, heads, poles)
- Paintbrushes (acrylic assortment of 1" to 4")
- Stir sticks
- Roller trays
- Tray liners
- Ladder (or stepladder)
- Brush cleaning comb (or wire brush)
- Paint remover
- Cotton rags
- Rubber gloves
- Flat razor scrapers
- Lightweight surfacing compound
- Putty knives
- Sandpaper/orbital sander
- Drywall patches
- Latex caulk
- Painter's tape (optional)
- Primer (optional)

TO PRIME OR NOT TO PRIME

Primer is a base coat of neutral white paint used to cover the existing wall color. It's useful if your walls have a glossy finish, because it can help flat paint adhere better to that surface. It also helps quiet an old, bold color that might alter the tone of a new, lighter color. But using primer adds a step that takes up precious time, so Clean Sweepers advise that you prime only when you have to. If possible use two coats of your chosen color instead. If priming is a must, ask the paint shop to tint the primer with your new color to give yourself a head start.

STEP 3 GET PAINTING!

To save time, the *Clean Sweep* crew doesn't tape off their makeover rooms; instead, they do touch-ups later. They suggest you start with doors, built-ins, and trim (wood borders such as the baseboards and door and window frames), painting with a brush, and then move on to large areas. Why? Brush-painting detailed areas such as trim is the most time-consuming part of the job but the easiest to touch up. Next "cut in" (or outline) the large remaining areas; use a small paintbrush—to reach the tight spots a roller can't get to—and then fill in the empty spaces with a roller. Roll on the paint in large Xs, repeating this pattern until the roller needs more paint. Continue until the room is covered completely with one coat. Let the first coat dry, then repeat the X-pattern step. Finally, survey the room for problem spots and touch up any splatters or bare patches with a small paintbrush.

STEP 4 MAKE IT PRETTY

Keep busy while the paint dries. There is no other time you'll have such easy access to the room's every nook and cranny, so start cleaning! A good scrub-down helps protect your paint job, because drying fans can send dust flying onto wet, freshly painted walls. Before you fire up the fans, clean windows, blinds, mirrors, fixture plates, fan blades, and even lightbulbs. Vacuum carpets and rugs. Treat rug stains with removers and rent a wet-vac to steam-clean worn-out carpet that can't be removed. (If you can't restore or remove a carpet, clean it and cover the offensive part with an area rug.) Vacuum or sweep and mop bare floors, using a disinfectant cleaner. After the space is spotless, turn on ceiling or portable area fans, open windows, and let the room dry. Wash brushes and neatly store paint and brushes and, if you can, let the painted room dry overnight. The next day, mount the plates and any fixtures you may have taken down.

SHOW SECRETS

- Latex remover remedies accidental splatters and spills on carpet and more.

- Area fans speed up the drying process.

- Saturated, dark colors (such as rich reds) require several coats; extra coats cost more time and money.

▶ Two light coats dry faster than one heavy coat.

- Skip taping off areas to save time. (If you prefer to tape, use masking tape instead of painter's tape to save money.)

- If you tape off a room, run latex caulk along the edge of marked-off sections to seal the seam between colors; when you remove the tape, you'll have a crisp line.

- Let paint dry overnight before you work on the rest of a room.

- Let the first coat dry completely before you add a second coat.

- Latex paint dries faster than oil-base paint.

- Flat finishes hide wall imperfections; glossy finishes highlight irregularities.

▶ Save leftovers for touch-ups. Record the brand and color number in case you need to buy more for later repairs.

- Paint interior closet walls to give your organization hub a fresh look.

- If removing wallpaper is a must, douse the paper with removing solution and let it thoroughly soak in before peeling off the wallpaper.

PAINT: BEDROOM

PROBLEM: Blue walls and rainbow-color door and window frames were fun, but the mismatching hues created disharmony and interrupted the visual flow of the space.

SOLUTION: Choosing a bold green that was both soothing and exciting gave the room a unified look and an even-keeled vibe. Wall-mounted votives add a moody glow.

BACKGROUND: A happily married couple inhabited this bedroom—a certified disaster area. The duo, performers who do an Ike and Tina Turner tribute show, stored their costumes, their everyday clothes, and piles of electronics in the same space, making the room feel like a stressed-out closet. They craved romance and serenity, *plus* the bold and the beautiful, and Molly fulfilled their wacky wishes with a funky, functional space awash with color.

PROBLEM: The cool curvy headboard went unnoticed amid the clutter. Metallic silver linens seemed cold and uninviting.

SOLUTION: Molly traced the headboard and painted tonal stripes to mimic its curve and emphasize its shape. She used faux-fur fabric, which complements the paint colors, to make the bed cozy and welcoming.

PAINT: **OFFICE**

PROBLEM: Most offices typically feel bland because functionality dictates they house the predictable—a desk, chairs, computer, clock, and shelving.

SOLUTION: James used color to make this work space invigorating. On one wall he painted a plaid design to create a focal point and tied the pattern to the rest of the room with a red panel that acts as a wainscot.

BACKGROUND: Originally, the sterile, white room was a pile-magnet for this family of four. Intended as an office and crafting studio for the parents, it had become a messy mayhem of empty boxes and knickknacks. Because there was so much toss-worthy junk all over the floor, the mom had even broken a toe trying to navigate the space. Post-purge, James used paint to add oomph to the space and give it a unified, efficient, and orderly feel. The crisp lines and bold color-blocking make sloppiness a near impossibility.

PROBLEM: Because she had no space in the office, the mom had to do her scrapbooking on a coffee table in another room. Instead of moving the other table into this sleek, new office, she needed a dedicated spot of her own.

SOLUTION: Because scrapbooking is this mom's part-time hobby, it didn't merit taking over the whole room. So Eric built a supply cabinet that rolls out on casters to form a desk when the creative urge strikes. Painting it black made it look compact and worked with the other new computer desk.

PROBLEM: Paperwork and files tend to be white and creams, thus unorganized mounds can easily blend into the background of neutral or unpainted offices and office furniture.

SOLUTION: Choosing bold colors for the walls and dark colors for the furniture means clutter stands out, which inevitably acts as a deterrent for building up more piles.

PROBLEM: White walls contributed nothing to this space and dirtied easily from the touch of little hands. All the empty wall space made the room seem overwhelming.

SOLUTION: Introducing vibrant new paint colors added visual interest to the walls. Eric mounted basketball goals on the wall and built open, netted boxes below, so storing toys becomes a hoops game. Sports equipment stowed in gym bags and hung on the wall provides order and frees up floor space.

BACKGROUND: This was an immaculate house…except for two rooms, including a bland catchall basement that housed sports and exercise equipment, a spare mattress, and odds and ends galore. The family's two little boys (and their cousins right around the corner) needed room to run. Molly created a playroom with pizzazz, where organization is interactive and bold stripes tie together a once-sprawling space.

PROBLEM: The existing stairway was unsound, unsafe, and somewhat disconnected from the rest of the room.

SOLUTION: Eric added a sturdy stair rail that echoes the wall stripes, and Molly continued the paint pattern along the stair wall to create visual harmony.

CHAPTER 7

FIT
FURNITURE

On the show, function always outweighs fashion and sentimental attachments, and furniture is not exempt from scrutiny. *Clean Sweep* designers have to identify "healthy" furniture in an instant and come up with remedies to save the sickly pieces. Attend this brief session of Furniture 101 to learn how to spot the keepers.

WHAT'S DEFUNCT?

Furniture past its prime has to go. If the overall structure is unsound, if the drawers don't open and close, if it's a prefab piece that's falling apart, it's not a keeper, says Angelo. Molly agrees: To be a keeper, a piece must have integrity. If it's an inexpensive, unsturdy, mass-made piece, haul it to the curb.

WHAT CAN LEAD A DOUBLE LIFE?

If you have a sturdy, serviceable coffee table with a surface that has seen better days, rethink its original use. In one *Clean Sweep* episode, the family needed a footrest in the living room, so Molly stapled a foam cushion onto their coffee table, pulled a slipcover over the altered piece, and voilà—they had an ottoman. The slipcover reached to the floor, so it concealed storage containers hidden underneath. Follow Molly's lead and challenge every bit of furniture to have a job. If it can serve more than one purpose, all the better. Be creative: Can an old wardrobe house your TV and sound system? Can a short bookshelf double as a nightstand? Can two short filing cabinets serve as the legs to a desk? Can a chest be a settee, a coffee table, or an ottoman? Think in terms of storage and accent piece and you're on the right track.

WHAT'S REVIVABLE?

If you have furniture that's solid in structure, useful overall, but looking a bit tired, give it a makeover. Paint it (glossy white always freshens a piece) and add new pulls and hardware and you'll have a like-new piece. If you decide to paint stained pieces, strip and sand the old finish first. To paint laminated pieces, use a special deglossing primer first (check with home improvement centers for recommendations). If you can't integrate an heirloom or antique into your new room design, give it to a relative or a friend who will cherish it.

This file cabinet ended up a keeper because it efficiently stores the homeowner's art photos and it works with the den's decor. Its bulk anchors the corner and the shelf above, and its clean lines and neutral color blend with the other furniture. To soften the unit's overall utilitarian look, Kelli topped it off with flowers and books.

ERIC'S EASIEST BUILDS

Two priceless pieces of highly functional furniture for under $50? Fabulous. Any novice can tackle these projects, rumored to be the easiest builds in the world from Eric Stromer's Signature Simpleton Series. Take Eric's advice and let the lumber store cut the pieces for you. It makes life easier.

CLOSET DESK $15 AND 15 MINUTES

MATERIALS

- **Three 1×2 boards (These are the braces: 1 piece for each side of the closet and the third for the back wall of the closet.)**
- **Plywood or other sheetlike board 1 to 2 inches thick (This is the desk top.)**
- **One 1×2 board (This is the front edge of the desk, a finishing touch.)**
- **Nails**
- **Paint**
- **Hammer**
- **Tape measure**
- **Level**
- **Sandpaper**
- **Polyurethane spray**

STEP 1 Measure your closet and have all lumber materials cut to suit the dimensions.

STEP 2 Sand and paint the plywood and the decorative 1×2. When they are completely dry, spray polyurethane on the top and front for a polished surface.

STEP 3 Nail each of the three 1×2 braces 30 inches up from the floor in the closet. One piece should be placed horizontally on the back wall, and the two remaining pieces should be similarly mounted opposite each other. Check that all of them are level.

STEP 4 Nail the decorative 1×2 across the outward-facing edge of the plywood.

STEP 5 Place the plywood across the braces, finished edge facing out.

BOOKSHELF A NO-BRAINER

MATERIALS

- **Six 1×12 boards (1 piece for the top; 1 equal piece for the bottom; 2 equal pieces for sides; 2 pieces 1 inch shorter than the top and bottom pieces for shelves)**
- **¼-inch luaun for backing**
- **Nails**
- **Wood glue**
- **Paint**
- **Level**
- **Sandpaper**
- **Polyurethane spray**
- **Hammer**
- **Tape measure**

STEP 1 Measure to determine the desired height and width of the unit. Have the 1×12s and the luaun cut to suit the dimensions.

STEP 2 Sand and paint all pieces. Apply polyurethane.

STEP 3 Have a helper hold the two side pieces upright on a worktable. Run wood glue across the tops. Place the top board across the two sides. Nail the top to the sides at each corner.

STEP 4 Flip the piece over and attach the bottom board to create a fully framed box. (See Step 3 for procedure.)

STEP 5 Place the shelves at the desired height and check that they are level. Nail them into place from the outer face of the joining board, using one nail at each corner of the shelf.

STEP 6 Run wood glue along the outer edge of one side of the frame and attach the luaun as backing. Nail at intervals along all four sides to secure.

PROBLEM: A wall of sliding closet doors allowed the couple to stash and hide loads of clutter. The wall of doors made the room claustrophobic and dysfunctional.

SOLUTION: Removing the closet doors opened up the room and made it easier to access the shelving. Painting the wall behind the shelves, adding stylish storage boxes, and hanging clothes by color made this an attractive, soothing, and hardworking area rather than an eyesore.

BACKGROUND: This office space held collectibles, clothes, and scrapbook supplies, but it was such a mess that neither drawers nor closet doors would close. After the homeowners downsized their piles and organized the keepers, Angelo restocked the newly serene space, making it a place where they could craft, work, or kick back.

PROBLEM: Superfluous electronics covered the desk and made it impossible for the wife to do her scrapbooking. The husband's professional and personal mementos were hidden under piles of unidentified objects.

SOLUTION: Eric built a separate desk for each person, and Angelo placed their frequently used items within easy reach. Cherished mementos were framed and hung on the walls, and favorite collectibles were placed on shadowbox shelves, where they will get due attention.

"NO MATTER HOW GREAT YOU THINK A FURNITURE PIECE IS, IF YOU DON'T USE IT, IT'S NOT THAT GREAT. DON'T BOTHER WASTING YOUR TIME TRYING TO MAKE IT WORK IF IT DOESN'T SERVE A PURPOSE FOR YOU, OR IF THERE'S SIMPLY NO ROOM FOR IT."

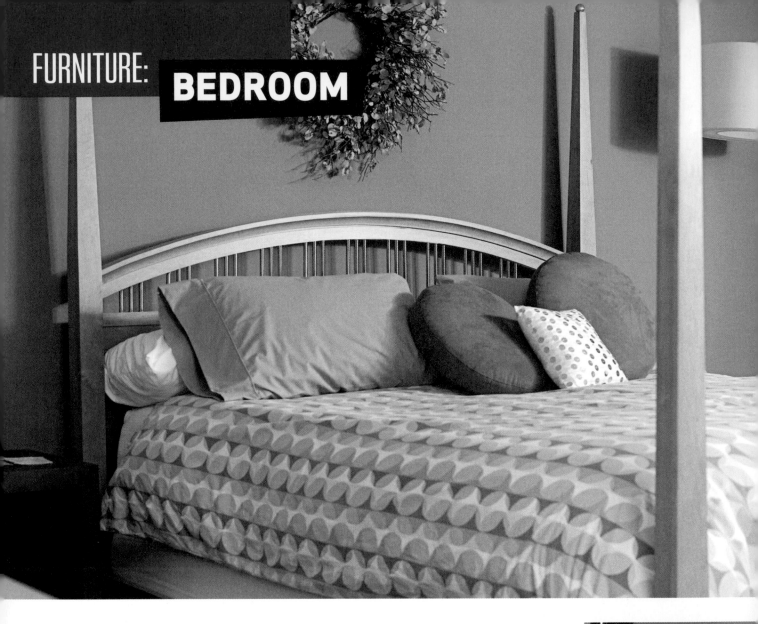

FURNITURE: BEDROOM

BACKGROUND: Because the family office was so crammed with clutter, paperwork overflowed into the couple's bedroom, where it was stuffed under the furniture. Clothing spilled out of the chest of drawers, and a giant playpen served as a laundry bin. After putting the paperwork in its proper place and culling their clothes to suit the space, Kelli made the couple's bedroom a tranquil getaway with storage aplenty.

PROBLEM: The old shelf system didn't maximize the closet's vertical space, and the door stayed open, eating up wall space.

SOLUTION: New shelves were added along the right wall in the closet to take advantage of its depth. To save space, the door was replaced with a curtain that matches the window treatments.

"I LIKE TO DESIGN ROOMS AROUND COLOR—IT NEVER FAILS ME AND I LOVE TO THROW IT AROUND A ROOM. THAT APPROACH—PAINT COLOR FIRST, THEN ART AND LINENS NEXT—ALWAYS MAKES A SPACE COME TOGETHER."

PROBLEM: Even after their purge and sort, the couple needed more storage room for remaining clothes and sundries. They also needed somewhere to sit in the room other than on the bed.

SOLUTION: Eric built two bedside tables so each person has a place to store personal belongings. Kelli converted an existing chest into a love seat by topping it with a seat cushion and custom monogrammed pillow.

MONOGRAMMED PILLOW

HOW-TO

TOOLS NEEDED

- ▶ Tape measure
- ▶ Scissors or rotary cutter and self-healing cutting mat
- ▶ Iron and ironing board
- ▶ Vanishing-ink pen
- ▶ Ruler or letter stencil
- ▶ Bleach pen
- ▶ Straight pins
- ▶ Sewing machine
- ▶ Hand-sewing needle

MATERIALS NEEDED

- ▶ ½ yard fabric, purple or desired color
- ▶ Matching thread
- ▶ 12×12-inch pillow form
- ▶ Monofilament thread
- ▶ Kraft paper

STEP 1

Machine wash the fabric; do not use fabric softener. Dry the fabric. Cut two pieces of fabric, each 13 × 13 inches; press.

STEP 2

Lay kraft paper on your work surface. Select one piece of fabric as the pillow front and lay it right side up on the kraft paper. Using a vanishing-ink pen and a ruler, draw the desired letter onto the fabric (see A and B). (If you prefer, use a stencil to create your monogram.) When you are satisfied with your design, trace the outline of the monogram with a bleach pen; let dry. (**Note:** The bleached areas will not turn white; after drying, the monogram outline will be lighter than the fabric.) Machine wash the pillow front; do not use fabric softener. Press the pillow front.

STEP 3

Lay the pillow front right side up on your work surface. Place the pillow back on the pillow front, right side down, aligning the edges. Pin and stitch around three sides, using a ½-inch seam allowance. Turn right side out. Insert the pillow form into the cover. Slip-stitch the opening closed, using monofilament thread and the hand-sewing needle.

A

B

FUNCTION: LAUNDRY ROOM

PROBLEM: Clean and dirty clothes mingled in hampers and sat sloppily on the dryer because there was no designated folding space in the laundry room.

SOLUTION: Eric built a laundry folding table that runs the length of one wall; Angelo placed it next to the dryer so Mom can pull out clean clothes and fold them immediately. Storage space below houses linens on one side and crafts items on the other. When it's project time, the ironing pad comes off, leaving a spacious work area.

BACKGROUND: Two parents with three sons and two full-time jobs equaled a laundry fiasco in this household. Forget piles—they had mountains of the smelly stuff. Because Mom tackles 10 to 12 loads at a time, she needed an efficient setup to facilitate the chore. Angelo gave her a streamlined space, and because the room was half playroom, he camouflaged the laundry area with curtains.

PROBLEM: When clothes aren't folded and put away as soon as they are clean, laundry rooms become closets.

SOLUTION: Mom made a rule for herself: She can close these curtains only if there are no clothes in sight. Thus the curtains do their job—they hide laundry machines, not laundry mess.

LAUNDRY FOLDING TABLE

HOW-TO

TOOLS NEEDED

- ▶ Table saw or circular saw
- ▶ Tape measure
- ▶ Combination square
- ▶ Finish nailer or hammer
- ▶ Screwdriver
- ▶ Nail set
- ▶ Paintbrushes and rags
- ▶ Safety goggles

MATERIALS NEEDED

- ▶ Three 4×8-foot sheets $3/4$-inch plywood
- ▶ Two 4×8-foot sheets $1/2$-inch plywood
- ▶ One 4×8-foot sheet $1/4$-inch hardboard
- ▶ 9 feet of 1×2-inch lumber
- ▶ $18^1/2$ feet of 2×2 lumber
- ▶ 12 feet of $1/4$×2-inch lattice molding
- ▶ Nails: 6d finishing, 4d finishing, 4d box
- ▶ Wood glue
- ▶ 3 pair hidden cabinet door hinges and 3 door pulls
- ▶ Primer
- ▶ 1 gallon semigloss paint
- ▶ Adjustable shelf standards

STEP 1

Cut the following from $3/4$-inch plywood:
2 end panels 31×$23^7/8$ inches
top and bottom $70^1/2$×$23^7/8$ inches
2 dividers $29^1/2$×$23^7/8$ inches
3 shelves $23^7/8$×23 inches
3 leg tops $23^7/8$×6 inches
6 leg sides $23^7/8$×$2^1/4$ inches
3 leg fronts 6×3 inches
Cut the following from $1/2$-inch plywood:
3 doors 31×$23^7/8$ inches
tabletop 76×26 inches
Cut from straight, knot-free 1×2 lumber:
top front edge $74^1/2$ inches
2 top end edges 26 inches
Cut from straight, knot-free 2×2 lumber:
tabletop back support $74^1/2$ inches
2 tabletop center supports $23^1/8$ inches
4 tabletop end supports 25 inches
Cut from hardboard:
back 72×31 inches

STEP 2

To assemble the cabinet, glue and nail the end panels to the bottom, butting the inside face of the end panel against the end of the bottom. The smooth face of the end panels should face out; the smooth surface of the bottom should face up. Drive 6d finishing nails through the end panels into the bottom panel.

STEP 3

To create the center shelf section, center one shelf on one divider panel. Check that the divider is square with the shelf; then glue and nail the shelf to the panel. Glue and nail the remaining divider to the opposite edge of the shelf, making an H-shape unit (see A, B, and C).

STEP 4

Center the divider/shelf assembly on the bottom piece and glue and nail it in place (see D). Glue and nail the top to the dividers and end pieces. Glue and nail the back to all back edges using 4d box nails.

STEP 5

For the legs, glue and nail two leg sides to each leg top (see E). Glue and nail a leg front to each leg. Position the legs on the bottom of the cabinet, centering one and allowing the legs at each side to extend 2 inches beyond the ends of the cabinet (see F). Glue and nail, using short 4d finishing nails (so they won't penetrate into the cabinet interior).

STEP 6

Glue and nail the 1×2 front and end edges to the underside of the tabletop (the smooth side of the plywood should be faceup). Referring to the diagram *at right* for positioning, glue and nail the 2×2 tabletop back support to the top of the cabinet so the back edge of the 2×2 is flush with the cabinet back. The ends will extend $1^{1}/_{4}$ inches beyond the ends of the cabinet. Attach tabletop center supports to the cabinet top, centering them over the dividers. Glue and nail tabletop end supports on the cabinet top at the front edge and between front and back supports. Fit the tabletop over the supports; glue and nail it in place. Trim the edges of the tabletop with 2-inch lattice molding.

STEP 7

Sand, prime, and paint the entire cabinet and doors. Let dry. Attach the doors to the cabinet with hidden cabinet hinges, following the manufacturer's instructions. Install pulls. Install adjustable shelf standards for side-section shelves.

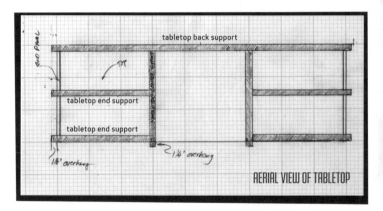

AERIAL VIEW OF TABLETOP

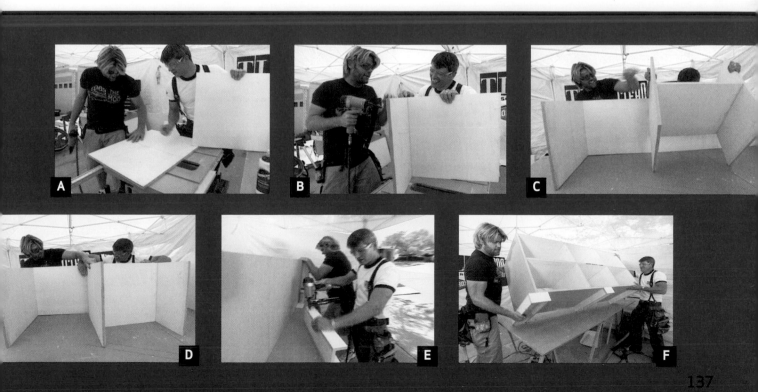

137

PART 4

ORGANIZE YOUR WORLD

Putting *Clean Sweep* into practice doesn't end when the cameras switch off. After all, organization is a way of life. To set yourself up for long-term success, it's essential to invest in quality storage solutions, and to adopt the proper patterns of behavior. But living the clean life is not necessarily just another chore. In fact, it can be an inspiring way of life. Consider this:

When the *Clean Sweep* crew finishes a makeover, the trucks that pick up the yard sale leftovers for charity donations don't arrive for at least another two days. Why the delay? "People usually get inspired to *Clean Sweep* the rest of their house," says show producer Susan Seide. Apparently their immaculate rooms outshine the rest of the house, and homeowners can't stomach the disharmony. Could this happen to you? Read on to learn how to get on the storage bandwagon and stay there.

CHAPTER 8

SALVATION THROUGH STORAGE

"A place for everything and everything in its place" is another *Clean Sweep* mantra that Peter and the rest of the clutter-phobic cast try to hammer into homeowners' heads. To create and maintain such order, it's essential to have top-notch storage systems and supplies. Refer to chapter 4: Function Rules (pages 66–83) for directions on laying out a perfect closet; use the following strategies to outfit the rest of your space for utmost organization.

KNOW WHAT TO STOW

"One of the biggest mistakes people make is to pile clutter on any empty surface," says Kelli. To decide what goes in a drawer versus on a desk top, what goes in a closet versus out on a bookshelf, ask yourself what you use most often. Assign those items a "Level One" importance and follow suit for the remainder of the keepers in the space, giving higher numbers to things used less often. Next, remember your room zones—the different activity areas you established in the space. Place relevant items in the proper zone, putting the lowest-numbered items within the easiest reach, the highest numbers in more remote spots, such as top closet shelves, under-the-bed boxes, and so forth.

CLIMB THE WALLS

There are certain tried-and-true tricks of the tidy trade that the *Clean Sweep* cast employs on nearly every episode. One favorite? Climbing the walls. Look at the images throughout this book and you'll see the evidence. Hanging bars affixed to walls become magazine racks; bikes cling to ceiling hooks; suspended shelves appear in a myriad of shapes, sizes, and configurations, all in an effort to give everything a specific, orderly home. Look at bare walls in your space and ask yourself if they too might have storage potential.

REACH FOR THE BEST

When you're micro-organizing, Peter suggests you play car driver to figure out where to stash things. "A driver," he says, "is stationary but can still reach the wheel, pedals, gears, stereo, controls, and more from the driver's seat. Similarly, you should be able to easily reach any items you use daily."

PERFECT CONTAINER

Choose containers that suit the style of your room—fabrics and wickers for traditional spaces; crisp metals and plastics for modern ones—and open your mind to materials such as leather, canvas, metal, and dressed-up cardboard. To get the best container for the job, keep these "shoulds" in mind:

▶ Containers should make full use of the depth and height of a storage area.

▶ Items should fit inside containers with room to spare, or at least without cramming.

▶ Lids should seal tightly and open easily.

▶ Containers should be see-through or clearly labeled to facilitate efficient access.

▶ Boxes should be sturdy enough to withstand the use they'll get.

▶ Clothing should be stored in canvas or cloth bags because plastic bags can damage clothes.

▶ Photos should be kept in acid-free boxes for protection.

THINK OUTSIDE THE

Peter and the designers are always looking for innovative storage ideas, whether they're trolling office supply or hardware stores, kitchen shops, or other venues. The trick is to see things based on your needs rather than the original intended use. Here are some examples of clever repurposing:

- ▶ **Use a kitchen utensil organizer** as a desk drawer organizer

- ▶ **Use a galvanized water bucket** as an art supply bucket

- ▶ **Use a blank price tag with string ties** as a bin label

- ▶ **Use a bike wall hook** as a guitar and snowboard hook

- ▶ **Use an antique suitcase** as a photo album holder

- ▶ **Use a photo box** as a CD holder

"CONTAINERS SHOULD FIT THE DECOR AND YOUR VISION FOR THE ROOM OR SPACE." —Peter

This is especially important if you're organizing a desk, workstation, or crafts area. Place everything you need from minute to minute in your primary zone, says Peter. Put things that you use frequently but less often in a secondary reach zone, within stretching distance. Last, he says, store things you need only every now and then in the same zone, but in an area a few steps away. Design your space to cater to your particular needs and you'll keep it tidy with little effort.

SHELVE IT

Shelves are for filing your belongings in plain sight, and the setup must be orderly to qualify as clutter-free. On the show, Clean Sweepers always fight the clock, so their favorite shelf systems are the easy-to-assemble variety. The team swears by prefab boxed wire sets (hang one brace bar, hook on shelf and drawer elements, and you're done). For

RELOAD YOUR ROOM

After the paint has dried and the fixtures and furniture are in place, piece together your room the way Clean Sweepers do.

STEP 1
Set up new storage systems.

STEP 2 Prep items for restocking (wash and fold clothes, wipe down electronics, and organize office supplies, books, DVDs, and so on).

STEP 3
Place items in their new storage containers.

STEP 4
Label containers.

STEP 5
Return like items to the room one zone at a time.

FOUR STEPS TO FABULOUS FOLDING

Ever wonder how the *Clean Sweep* crew folds keeper clothes with such precision? The secret lies in folding boards like this one Peter found online. Track down a board of your own—online or at organization stores—and follow these steps for showroom-ready closets and drawers.

ONE Place a clean T-shirt front side down and centered on the board. Fold any bottom overhang upward, making the shirt's bottom edge even with the base of the board. Smooth out any wrinkles.

TWO Flip the right side of the board to the center to fold over one sleeve; then flip it back again. Repeat on the left side.

THREE Flip the bottom panel up and back again and voilà—you have a perfectly folded shirt.

FOUR Stack like shirts together and arrange them by color. Use clip-on shelf dividers (also found at organization stores) to keep stacks orderly and uniform.

custom jobs, Eric fashions basic shelves at the drop of a hard hat (see Eric's Easiest Builds, pages 126–127). Determine what's going where; then shop for the best bins for your buck, aiming for functional containers that look good too. Looks are important because they'll inspire you to maintain the new order.

KEEP KIDS IN MIND

The *Clean Sweep* team is adamant that kids should always play a role in keeping shared family spaces in order. To help them do their part, create storage that they can handle and access on their own. Label containers (tape photos, their names, or color-coded tags to bins so younger children can identify the contents) and place them within safe reach. If possible, make a game of it, as Molly often does. In one house, she put labeled tricycles and other riding toys in grown-up-style, labeled parking spaces. In another home she hung basketball goals in a rec room; when the boys toss their toys into the hoops, the toys land in custom-made bins below.

ORGANIZATION AND STORAGE TOOL KIT

- ▶ **Staple gun**
- ▶ **Containers**
- ▶ **Cord binders**
- ▶ **Drawer organizer**
- ▶ **File folders**
- ▶ **Filing cabinets**
- ▶ **Hooks**
- ▶ **Labels**
- ▶ **Label maker**
- ▶ **Laundry folding board**
- ▶ **Shelf-making or shelf assembly tools**
- ▶ **Shelf dividers**
- ▶ **Desktop supply holders**
- ▶ **Wooden hangers**

PROBLEM: An overflow of hobby electronics crowded the room and rendered the work space unusable. If the owner could find what he was looking for, he'd have to play contortionist to plug in the item.

SOLUTION: Vertical storage, much of it on the wall, frees up horizontal work space. Note the layers: The tower and keyboard sit below the desk top; a metal Peg-Board hangs on the wall and offers storage for business cards and miscellany; smart-looking containers top off a floating shelf that showcases important equipment.

BACKGROUND: This office space was overrun with electronics. Cables, empty equipment boxes, and collectible ham radios ruled the roost. In order to master the mania, Peter convinced the hobbyist to toss the excess, and Angelo devised a storage system that highlights the best of the leftovers.

PROBLEM: Because electronics took up much of the office space, household tasks such as bill paying grew disorganized. Credit card bills, for example, ended up on the floor.

SOLUTION: Filing cabinets, shelves filled with pertinent reference materials, and magazine holders brought order to house management chores.

WALL-MOUNTED SHELVES

TOOLS NEEDED

- ▶ Tape measure
- ▶ Stir sticks
- ▶ Table saw
- ▶ Paint tray
- ▶ Safety goggles
- ▶ Paintbrushes
- ▶ Finish nailer
- ▶ Stud finder
- ▶ Brad nailer

MATERIALS NEEDED

- ▶ 4×8-foot sheets ³⁄₄-inch MDF (medium-density fiberboard)*
- ▶ 4×8-foot sheets ³⁄₄-inch plywood*
- ▶ Wood glue
- ▶ 2-inch nails
- ▶ 1-inch brads
- ▶ Primer
- ▶ Latex paint, white and blue or other desired colors

*Purchase materials after determining finished size. See Steps 1 and 8.

STEP 1

Determine the size of your finished shelving unit, including the dimensions of each display slot and the overall length and height. **Note:** The shelf *opposite* has five 11-inch-square openings, each 8 inches deep. Adjust the dimensions of your shelving unit to fit your particular space.

STEP 2

Cut 10 pieces of MDF, each 8×11 inches. Cut four pieces of MDF, each 2×11 inches. Stand two 8×11-inch pieces of MDF upright on your work surface, with an 11-inch-long side up. Glue and then nail one 2×11-inch piece of MDF to the ends of the two upright pieces, lining up the edges (see A and B). Repeat to create four dividers, reserving the final two pieces of 8×11-inch MDF to create the shelf ends in Step 3.

STEP 3

Cut two pieces of MDF 8³⁄₄ ×64¹⁄₂ inches (or long enough to connect the shelving dividers created in Step 2), taking into account the width of each individual opening plus 2 inches for the width of each divider; also figure in an overhang of ³⁄₄ inch on each end. These pieces will serve as the top and bottom of the display slots. Lay the bottom piece on your work surface. Measuring carefully and spacing the dividers as desired, place each divider on the bottom piece. **Note:** Place all the dividers so that the 2-inch-wide front of each one faces the same direction (the front of the unit). Position the remaining two 8×11-inch MDF pieces from Step 2 on the bottom piece, placing them ³⁄₄ inch from the ends of the bottom piece (these pieces form the outer side of the first and fifth slots). Glue the bottom edges of the dividers onto the bottom piece, aligning edges; nail to secure. Flip over the unit and apply glue to the top edges of the dividers; place the top piece on top of the dividers, aligning edges. Nail the top piece in place.

STEP 4

Cut two pieces of MDF, each 8×15¹⁄₂ inches. Glue one 8×15¹⁄₂ piece to each end of the unit created in Step 3. There will be a scant ³⁄₄-inch gap between these end pieces and the end pieces attached in Step 3 (see C). Cut two pieces of MDF, each 2×15¹⁄₂ inches. Glue and then nail one 2×15¹⁄₂-inch piece to cover the ³⁄₄-inch gap so that the end pieces have a 2-inch-wide facing strip like the four dividers created in Step 2.

STEP 5

To face the top and bottom edges of the shelving unit, cut two pieces of MDF, each 2×60¹⁄₂ inches (or long enough to fit between the side facings applied in Step 4). Glue and then nail these pieces into place.

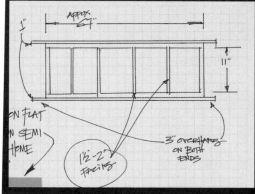

STEP 6

Cut two pieces of plywood 11³/₄ inches wide and 6 inches longer than the top and bottom pieces cut in Step 3. Glue and then nail the top piece to the top edges of the frame created in Step 5, allowing the top piece to overhang the unit by 3 inches on each side (see C). To prevent the plywood top from splitting, use brads to attach the top piece. Flip over the unit and attach the bottom piece with glue and brads, again allowing a 3-inch overhang on each side. **Note:** There should be a 1³/₄-inch gap between the top and bottom pieces attached in Step 3 and the top and bottom pieces just attached on the back side of the overall unit. These will allow for mounting the unit on the wall.

STEP 7

Prime the entire shelving unit; let dry. Paint the shelving unit in the desired colors; let dry. **Note:** The top and bottom strips of the unit shown are painted white, and the shelf openings and dividers are painted blue.

STEP 8

Rip two pieces of MDF, each 1¹/₂ inches wide and 1 inch shorter than the lengths cut in Step 3 (the top and bottom pieces). Using a stud finder, attach the two ripped pieces to the wall so that they will align with the 1³/₄-inch gaps on the back of the shelving unit. Slip the shelving unit onto the two ripped pieces of MDF. Using brads, attach the unit to the ripped pieces on the top and bottom.

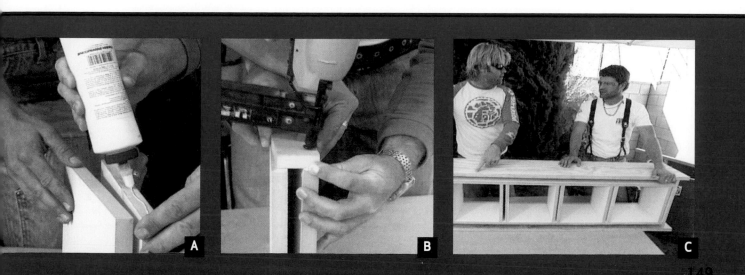

149

PROBLEM: This garage was Grand Central Storage for a home-based painting business. The proprietor, a husband and father, stored his equipment and tools in a haphazard fashion, so the place was a mess and no one in the house respected his belongings.

SOLUTION: Eric built a set of supply shelves and a sturdy worktable, topping off the latter with Peg-Board for vertical tool storage. Each element made Dad's work zone more functional and legitimized his job and his contribution to the family.

BACKGROUND: After merging their two families, the homeowners put all their overflow items into the garage "to deal with later." Later came when the car couldn't fit inside and when family members were embarrassed every time the garage door opened. Peter forced the parents to sort through Dad's paint business paraphernalia, Mom's exercise equipment, and the kids' odds and ends. Meanwhile Molly devised a color and storage scheme that tied together four separate activity zones. In the end, there was room for a workshop, a laundry station, and bike and car storage.

PROBLEM: The family's four kids tossed their bikes in tangled heaps, a habit that was dangerous for them and bad for the bikes.

SOLUTION: Molly placed a bike rack along one side of the garage, creating instant order. Hanging extra tires and rims on the wall reduces clutter on the floor.

PROBLEM: Mom hauled laundry piles to and from the facilities in the garage, an unpleasant chore that made skipping the folding stage an irresistible temptation. The drab environment didn't inspire cleanliness on anyone's part.

SOLUTION: Bright colors cheered up the space and motivated everyone to keep it clean. An open-shelved folding table, drying racks, and a roller basket made laundry a step-by-step affair.

BICYCLE HELMETS

PROBLEM: An exposed water heater contributed to the warehouse atmosphere, making the space feel like a storage unit rather than a family zone.

SOLUTION: Eric built a simple hinged Peg-Board screen to hide the water unit, and Peter placed all loose sports equipment in cabinets to maintain order. The cabinet doors keep balls away from the car, promoting safety.

MULTIPURPOSE TABLE WITH SHELF

TOOLS NEEDED

- ► Tape measure
- ► Table saw
- ► Safety goggles
- ► Finish nailer
- ► Stir sticks
- ► Paint tray
- ► Paintbrushes

MATERIALS NEEDED

- ► Two 4×8-foot sheets ¾-inch plywood
- ► 2-inch nails
- ► Peg-Board (see Step 5 for size)
- ► Primer
- ► Latex paint, orange or other desired color
- ► Wood glue

STEP 1

Determine the size of your finished table, including the overall height and width. **Note:** The table *opposite* is 3 feet tall, 5 feet long, and 2½ feet wide. The following instructions are for a table of these dimensions. Adjust the dimensions of your table to fit your particular space.

STEP 2

Cut a piece of plywood 60×30 inches for the tabletop. Cut eight pieces of plywood 3×35 inches for the legs. Glue and then nail together the long edges of two leg pieces to form an L shape. Repeat with the remaining six pieces. Glue and nail the legs to the bottom of the tabletop, aligning edges.

STEP 3

Cut two pieces of plywood 61½ ×3 inches and two pieces 30×3 inches; these pieces will serve as the facing for the tabletop. Glue and then nail the long facing pieces to the tabletop, aligning top edges; allow ¾ inch to extend beyond each end. Glue and then nail the short facing pieces to the tabletop, aligning top edges and fitting between the overhang of the long facing pieces.

STEP 4

Cut four pieces of plywood 57×2 inches; these pieces will form the long edges of the pegboard shelf frame. Glue and then nail together the long edges of two of the frame pieces to form an L shape. Repeat with the remaining two pieces. Glue and then nail the two frame pieces to the inside of the table legs, 12 inches above the ground; attach each piece so that the frame will support the pegboard. Cut four pieces of plywood 24×2 inches for the short edges of the pegboard shelf frame. Glue and then nail together the long edges of two of the frame pieces to form an L shape. Repeat with the remaining two pieces. Glue and then nail the two frame pieces to the inside of the table legs so that they fit between the long frame pieces.

STEP 5

Cut the pegboard to 57×27 inches. Prime the top of the pegboard; let dry. Paint the top of the pegboard; let dry. Place the painted pegboard on the frame created and attached in Step 4.

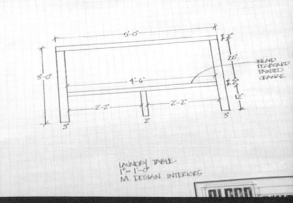

LAUNDRY TABLE
1" = 1'-0"
M. DESIGN INTERIORS

PROBLEM: Mirrored sliding doors are don'ts for two reasons: They look cold and can be difficult to close even when closets are in order.

SOLUTION: Molly sewed curtains that elegantly cover the newly organized closet space. Using fabric in place of the mirrors gave the room a warmer, softer feel.

BACKGROUND: The culprit behind this bedroom clutter was a mom who owned up to an addiction to clothes. She also owned a collection of exercise equipment that was gathering dust in the room. The space was such a mess, she and her husband did not want to sleep here. After a mega-purge, their keeper clothes finally fit their storage space. As for making the room a relaxing space for two? Molly saw to it, making sure the space provided the escape they both sought.

PROBLEM: Too many clothes and not enough storage space resulted in piles of clothes around the room. Surrounded by unused exercise equipment and clutter, the bed was not an inviting place to rest.

SOLUTION: Two new dressers, one for him (in the closet) and one for her (at the foot of the bed) give each person sufficient storage space. New wall color, art, and lamps make the bed a focal point and the room inviting.

CURTAINED DOORS

TOOLS NEEDED

▶ Tape measure

▶ Scissors or rotary cutter and self-healing cutting mat

▶ Straight pins

▶ Sewing machine

▶ Iron and ironing board

▶ Hook-and-loop tape

▶ Stud finder

▶ Electric screwdriver

MATERIALS NEEDED

▶ Fabric, white or other desired color for panel*

▶ Fabric, green or other desired color for border*

▶ Matching thread

▶ Curtain rod(s) and hanging hardware

* Purchase fabric after you have determined the finished size of your curtain panel.

STEP 1

To determine the finished size of each curtain panel, measure from the point where you plan to hang the curtain rod to the floor and add $2\frac{1}{4}$ inches. For the width, measure the width of the door frame and divide by 2 for a standard closet opening or by 4 for a double-width opening like the one *opposite*. Add 2 inches to the width measurement for each panel.

STEP 2

Cut the panel fabric to the length determined in Step 1 and the width minus 13 inches. **Note:** Each panel has a 6-inch-wide border on the long sides; the border is stitched to the

long sides of the panel with a $\frac{1}{2}$-inch seam in Step 3. Cut two border strips, each 7 inches wide and the length determined in Step 1 (see A).

STEP 3

Lay the panel fabric right side up. Pin one border strip to each long edge of the panel fabric, right sides together. Using a $\frac{1}{2}$-inch seam, stitch the border strips to the sides of the panel. Press the seams toward the border strips. Hem the sides and bottom of the finished panel with a $\frac{1}{2}$-inch hem (see B).

STEP 4

With the panel wrong side up, fold over the top edge $\frac{1}{4}$ inch; press. Fold the same edge over $1\frac{1}{2}$ inches; press. Edgestitch close to the first ($\frac{1}{4}$-inch) fold to form the bottom of the rod pocket. Topstitch $\frac{1}{4}$ inch from the second fold to form the top of the rod pocket. **Note:** Adjust the size of the rod pocket if your chosen rod is significantly larger or smaller. Repeat Steps 2 to 4 to create the remaining panels.

STEP 5

Attach the curtain rod hardware to the wall in the desired location; if possible, attach the hardware to the wall studs. Thread the curtain panels onto the rods; hang.

STEP 6

For the tie, cut one piece of white fabric 3×10 inches. Hem the short (3-inch) sides of the fabric, using a $\frac{1}{2}$-inch hem. With right sides together, stitch the long (10-inch) sides of the fabric, using a $\frac{1}{2}$-inch seam to form a tube. Turn the fabric right side out. Stitch the ends of the tube closed. Cut a piece of hook-and-loop tape approximately $1\frac{1}{2}$ inches long. Stitch one half of the tape to one end of the tie, about $\frac{1}{4}$ inch from the edges. Stitch the other half of the tape to the opposite end of the tie so that the tie can be secured around the panel. Repeat the entire process for each tie.

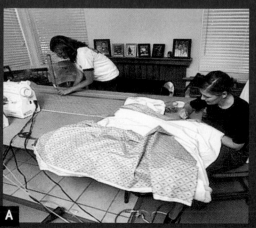

A

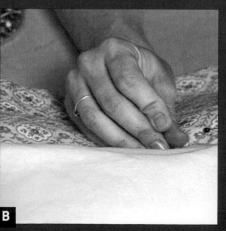

B

CHAPTER 9

MESS MAGNETS

Certain areas are perpetual danger zones for even the most devoutly reformed clutterbug. And certain items can lure any onetime collector into an impulse purchase. Let's face it, these mess magnets will always hold some temptation...but there is hope. The advice in this chapter will help you stay on your clean-swept path.

CLOTHES AND CLOSETS

DO: Use a combination of hanging racks, shelves, shelf dividers, and two-tiered rods, configuring them to suit the contents of your closet.

DO: Hang dressy clothes and fold knits to preserve the condition and shape of the garments.

DO: Organize ties and belts on racks.

DO: Invest in wooden hangers for a uniform look.

DO: Keep seasonal clothes within easy reach and store out-of-season clothes out of reach.

DO: Keep clothes off the floor and the furniture.

Hang all your clothes in one direction at the start of a season. When you wear an item, reverse the direction of the hanger. By season's end, you'll see what you've worn—and not worn. Get rid of the neglected clothes.

"WE WEAR 20 PERCENT OF OUR CLOTHES 80 PERCENT OF THE TIME." —*Peter*

CRAFTS AND SCRAPBOOKS

DO: Keep only those crafts materials relevant to the projects you have worked on in the past year.

DO: Purge old supplies from neglected projects.

DO: Have a definite purpose and timeline before starting a new project.

DO: Finish one project before starting a fresh one.

DO: Put away all materials after each crafting session.

TOP TIP: Set a limit for the number of projects you are working on at a single time.

"LIMITS, PHILANTHROPY, GENEROSITY, SHARING, ECONOMICS...YOU CAN TEACH YOUR CHILDREN ALL OF THOSE WITH TWO BINS OF TOYS." —*Peter*

TOYS

DO: Keep only what you have room for.

DO: Purge toys regularly, considering age appropriateness, use, and space.

DO: Get rid of broken toys.

DO: Set limits on the number of toys coming into your house.

DO: Tell gift givers your family's toy limits.

DO: Let your child choose a charity for donating old toys.

DO: Teach children to put away their own toys.

DO: Create storage that kids can reach themselves.

TOP TIP: Allow a finite amount of space—two bins, three buckets, etc.—for toy storage. When the space is full, ask your children to give up something old before bringing in anything new.

BOOKS AND BOOKSHELVES

DO: Allow more space than you think you need for books.

DO: Place some books horizontally, others vertically on a shelf for visual appeal.

DO: Use heavy objects such as vases or other items as bookends.

DO: Group books logically so you can find them quickly and easily.

DO: Purge your shelves of reference books and travel books every few years, because they become outdated.

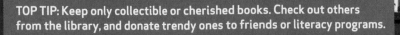

TOP TIP: Keep only collectible or cherished books. Check out others from the library, and donate trendy ones to friends or literacy programs.

BILLS AND FILING CABINETS

DO: Create or buy a filing system that divides your papers into categories.

DO: Keep unpaid bills in a central location.

DO: File bills after they are paid.

DO: Keep a year's worth of bills in an active file, rotating out the oldest month when you add a new month.

DO: Refer to the list on page 53 for guidelines on how long to keep bills and records.

DO: Clean out all files every 6 to 12 months, if not more often.

DO: Store files and bills away from your bedroom for a better night's sleep.

TOP TIP: If possible, pay bills online and store your records on a CD.

> "ONLY 20 PERCENT OF WHAT'S FILED EVER SEES THE LIGHT OF DAY. KNOW WHAT'S IN YOUR FILES AND USE THEM." —*Peter*

MAIL

DO: Throw out junk mail as soon as you walk in the door.

DO: Separate bills from other keeper mail.

DO: Keep bills in your bill-paying zone and file them after payment.

DO: Keep only sentimental letters—and file those in albums.

DO: Use a shredder to dispose of old letters, bills, and sensitive junk mail. If information stored on CDs becomes outdated, destroy the CDs.

TOP TIP: Place a trash can by your door for junk mail. Add a box or bin for incoming mail within a few steps.

FIVE CLUTTER-CUTTING RULES TO LIVE BY

1. Don't shop when you're bored.

2. Don't buy something just because it's on sale.

3. Practice the "one in, one out rule" on a daily basis.

4. Out of sight is not out of mind. Check boxes and files once a season—or at least once a year—to purge anew.

5. Make every new item brought into your house pass the keeper test (see page 47).

"THE LINE BETWEEN SOMETHING THAT'S COLLECTIBLE AND CLUTTER IS MICROTHIN." —*Peter*

SHOES

DO: Establish a set number of shoes to keep in your designated shoe storage space.

DO: Keep—at most—two of the same kind of shoe (athletic, dress, work, etc.) at any one time.

DO: Store shoes on shoe racks and in hideaway bins.

DO: Put shoes away after taking them off.

TOP TIP: Consider placing a bench and shoe storage system where shoes used to pile up.

MISCELLANEOUS SUPPLIES AND DRAWERS

DO: Use cutlery trays to organize supplies in desk drawers.

DO: Purge and sort through any drawer that won't close easily.

DO: Keep like items in the same drawer.

DO: Use drawers for storing specific items, not as a catchall or a trash bin.

TOP TIP: Cull excess and wayward, unnecessary items from drawers regularly.

DVDS, CDS, AND VIDEOTAPES

DO: Rent movies when possible.

DO: Buy only what you have room for.

DO: Download music instead of buying CDs.

DO: Upgrade from videotapes and cassettes to CD, DVD, and MP3 players to save space.

TOP TIP: Keep track of the movies you watch and CDs you listen to each year. Get rid of those you haven't used in the past 12 months.

PHOTOS

DO: Separate loose photos into eras of your life.

DO: Keep photos in albums.

DO: Discard doubles and images of poor quality.

DO: Set a limit on the number of photo albums you'll keep.

DO: Give children their own childhood albums when they move away from home.

TOP TIP: Get rid of negatives you don't need; scan images or keep a CD instead.

MEMORABILIA/ COLLECTIBLES

DO: Cull your collection so it includes only the best, most sentimental pieces.

DO: Perform the dust test regularly to check if you are respecting your collection.

DO: Honor your mementos by pulling out one item of import and framing it or showcasing it specially.

DO: Make a photo album of mementos you can't keep for lack of room.

DO: Get rid of the collection if your passion for it fades.

TOP TIP: Base the size of your collection on the space you have to display it.

CHAPTER 10

KEEP
IT CLEAN

"Clutter," says Peter, "keeps you in the past, steals physical space, and robs you of today." Accumulating stuff, he explains, is an attempt to hold on to memories, and to offset fears about not being prepared or needing something later. Within reason, memories and preparation are fine, but trouble sets in when you cross the line from Memory Lane and Preparation Alley into Clutterville. If you are struggling with letting go, reframe how you think. Focus instead on the life that you will bring to a suffocating space. Think of the shared family time to come and the peace of mind you'll gain when you live without clutter. It's about trading quantity of goods for quality of life, Peter says. To make that mental switch, practice these lessons learned.

LESSON 1 PRIORITIZE

"People often assign the same importance to everything," says Peter. For example, "Grandmother's diary about her travels in the Himalayas at the turn of the century is as important as the license plate off her car; and a photo of her and your grandfather is as important as an old pair of her boots. There's no way it's all equally important," he says. So keep the keepsakes and ditch the junk.

▶**LESSON LEARNED:** Separate meaningful mementos from old baggage. The rest? Let it go.

LESSON 2 HONOR YOUR MEMORIES

In one episode a couple owned a ton of sentimental LPs that belonged to the husband's grandmother. "But if they meant so much, why were they buried and covered in dust?" asks Peter. "I asked him to pick out two or three favorite records, and we framed those and hung them in his new office. Seeing them so powerfully honored made it easier for him to give up the rest. Instead of being a prisoner to the past, we refreshed the memory and brought it and him into the present. He was able to live organized and for today."

▶**LESSON LEARNED:** Pull out a few key items and display them in a way that respects both the past and the present. The rest? Let it go.

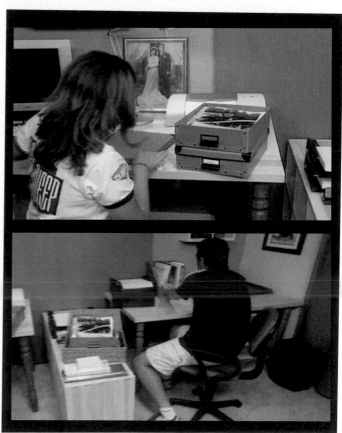

Choose matching boxes in a style that suits your decor to keep photos and other papers flat and dust-free. Tabs with labels let you find items quickly. It's a much more efficient system than rifling through drawers and cupboards in search of last year's vacation snaps.

LESSON 3 PLAY THE NUMBERS GAME

So you think letting go of something would be the worst thing in the world? "Draw up a list," says Peter, "numbered 0 to 10. Start at 10 and ask yourself what is the absolute worst thing that could possibly happen to you. Keep going on to number 0…what would it be—missing a meal? Losing $5? OK, where does your 'must-keep' item fit on the scale? Maybe it's at one and a half. Not so bad to lose it after all, now is it?"

▶**LESSON LEARNED:** The numbers don't lie. Stuff is never the most important thing in your world. Let it go.

GET MOTIVATED

SET YOURSELF SMALL GOALS. IF THE MAJOR GOAL IS TO EMPTY OUT A CLOSET, BREAK IT DOWN INTO SMALLER GOALS: MONDAY I'LL DO THE SHOES. TUESDAY I'LL DO BELTS AND ACCESSORIES. WEDNESDAY I'LL DO THE CLOTHES. WORKING ON SMALL CHUNKS IS A DEFINITE PLUS.

ADOPT NEW PATTERNS OF BEHAVIOR

Make organization part of your daily life so it becomes a mindless habit, not a dreaded chore. For example, put things away when you're done with them. Practice these easy behavior overhauls:

- ▶ When you take off your clothes, put them in the hamper or back in the closet.

- ▶ After showering, hang your towel.

- ▶ After eating, clean your dishes or put them in the dishwasher.

- ▶ When you take clothes out of the dryer, fold them immediately.

- ▶ If you have a recyclable item, put it in the recycle bin when you're done with it.

"WHY DO KIDS WHO GROW UP EATING SUSHI LIKE SUSHI AND ONES WHO GROW UP WITH FRIES LIKE FRIES? KIDS FOLLOW THEIR PARENTS' LEADS. IF YOU WANT YOUR CHILD TO LIVE AN UNCLUTTERED, ORGANIZED LIFE, YOU HAVE TO LIVE THE LIFE TOO." —Peter

LESSON 4   KEEP A LITTLE, GIVE A LOT

In one episode a tucked-away family painting turned up. The husband's mother had made it when she'd been diagnosed with cancer. The painting—a huge cityscape—had never been hung; it didn't work with the decor, and truth be told, there were other mementos that the couple was more attached to. The solution? They gave the painting to a relative. In other episodes, couples have taken photos of sentimental items before giving them up. Thus they downsize their clutter without losing the past.
▶**LESSON LEARNED:** Pass on any underappreciated item to those who are more apt to value, honor, and use it. In other words, let it go.

LESSON 5   RECYCLE

Another episode featured a family quilt that was no longer in use. Rather than get rid of the tattered blanket entirely, the designers used its scraps to make a keepsake album.
▶**LESSON LEARNED:** Look at an old item in a new light. Can you reincorporate your memory in a modern, organized way? If not, let it go.

LESSON 6   LIVE IN THE NOW

If it doesn't fit, if you don't wear it, if it's taking up room you don't have, get rid of it. That goes for the high school letter jacket, the hats that are collecting dust, your old wedding dress, and Halloween costumes you won't ever put on again.
▶**LESSON LEARNED:** Holding on to wearable nostalgia is a fashion don't. Make room for your current everyday clothes, and as for yesterday's style, let it go.

ALL FOR ONE AND ONE FOR ALL

When more than one person is living in clutter, more than one person is accountable for the disarray. After all, someone made the mess, and everyone else allowed it to be there. So quit the blame game and follow these tips for a successful *Clean Sweep*.

TIP 1 MAKE A CONTRACT.

Determine the purpose of your *Clean Sweep* with a group mission statement. Ask all those using the cluttered space to tell what they dream of for the room and what they are willing to do to achieve that vision and maintain it. Write a contract stating the shared vision, mission, and intentions and have everyone sign it. With a contract, you have buy-in from those who will be using the space in the future.

TIP 2 BE HONEST.

Getting rid of someone else's things on the sly is disrespectful and unfair. Let the owners of the items put their own stuff into a toss pile. If a shared item is disputed, make a team decision or follow input from your neutral third party (see page 48). If children are involved, the ultimate authority lies with the parents, but keep in mind that abusing the parent-knows-best privilege could set you up for a revolt down the road.

TIP 3 COMPROMISE.

One episode found two owners with similar items, both from before they lived together. Rather than picking one of the two to keep, both sold their items and used the profits to buy a replacement item together. If you reach such an impasse, take a breather and be rational. Meet in the middle for a happier home.

TIP 4 DON'T KEEP SCORE.

Sometimes it turns out that one person has to get rid of more things than another, but try to keep the sacrifices somewhat balanced. You got into this together, so it's important to get out of it together for future success and immediate harmony. The key to avoiding the win-lose trap? Don't rub anything in each other's face, and ask all parties to part with some favorite sentimental objects.

CLEAN: BEDROOM

BACKGROUND: The owners partially blamed their cluttered ways on a lack of color. "If there's no color in your house," explained the wife, "your home is bland and you tend to overcompensate, loading up with furniture and other stuff." After Angelo waltzed in and redid two rooms, the couple tackled the rest of the house on their own. Now there's not a white wall in the place, and the couple has made a habit of keeping everything pristinely clean.

PROBLEM: The room was part sleeping space, part crafting space. The two were locked in a messy war.

SOLUTION: Giving each keeper item its own spot allowed the color scheme to speak louder than the couple's stuff. Tucking scrapbook materials in discreet containers under the desk made it clear the room was first and foremost a haven.

BACKGROUND: When Angelo converted this spare room into a play space for a couple and their three young boys, the parents had to enforce strict rules to maintain the fresh look. "If you want to use the room," says Mom, "you've got to keep it clean. Otherwise you're not allowed in." Tough stuff, but the firm line works: The oldest son even monitors the younger two on his own, and the room has become a hot spot for game-playing and sleepovers. Would they invite Peter back for a surprise checkup? "Absolutely," everyone says. "Anytime!"

PROBLEM: Built-in cabinets in the playroom/laundry were greatly underutilized and nearly invisible against the all-white walls. Collectibles were scattered around the room, gathering dust and taking up precious floor space.

SOLUTION: Giving the room the primary designation of play space meant many of the collectibles had to go. Cleaned-out cabinets offered storage space for DVDs, CDs, and games. Painting the walls blue helped the room's white cabinets look crisp, clean, and orderly.

BACKGROUND: The skeleton in this family's closet was a downstairs guest room that was more dump than decor: Shower doors, boxes, and random clothes covered the bed and floor. Peter put an end to the piles, and Molly pulled the place together with a cheery yellow paint job that spread into the open closet. "Now," says the mom of the house, "we don't keep anything we don't use. And once a season we take time off to go through any buildup." Grandpa, a regular overnight guest, appreciates the hard work.

PROBLEM: The junky guest room was off-putting. It had no space for visitors, let alone their things.

SOLUTION: Removing the closet doors makes the room feel larger and enforces tidy habits because there are no doors to hide a mess. Adding an empty chest of drawers and spare hangers makes the space more welcoming.

CLEAN: LIVING ROOM

BACKGROUND: This living room was packed with exercise equipment, electronics, and remnants of unfinished renovation projects. After the family tossed loads of the stuff, Molly took her cue from their bold upholstered furniture and created a Moroccan look. The coat tree and a bench with built-in shoe storage keep the place looking neat and tidy.

PROBLEM: An imposing wall of electronics dominated the space, edging out quiet family activities.

SOLUTION: Establishing a cozy sitting space and a reading nook put family time and quiet endeavors first and brought life back into the living room.

CLEAN: OFFICE

PROBLEM: Crumbling concrete walls and low ceilings gave the space a dark, dank feel that made it easy to treat the room as second-class.

SOLUTION: Kelli was inspired by the space's utilitarian elements and created an industrial-looking space. She used sturdy indoor-outdoor carpet as flooring, sprayed gray paint on the walls to cover all the crevices and stop the crumbling, and opted for modern cabled glass shelves and stainless steel lighting to offset the rough texture of the walls. Upping the oo-la-la factor motivates the couple to keep it clean and has boosted their creative output.

BACKGROUND: A basement had become an out-of-sight, out-of-mind place to toss whatever couldn't fit upstairs in the home of this family of four. Scores of empty baskets, computer parts and cables, family knickknacks, and loads of tossables shared space with true heirlooms. When the husband—a graphic artist—added a gargantuan old-fashioned printing press to the mix, things had to change. After Peter got them to part with their unessential items, Kelli took a cue from their keepers and made the space part office, part print shop, and part studio. As for the husband and wife (a newspaper photographer), they were thrilled and now use the space to unleash their creativity.

PROBLEM: With so much junk in the room, it was only a matter of time before the type for the antique printing press was lost in the mess.

SOLUTION: By setting aside an area for the press itself and creating storage space for the boxes of type, the prized possession is properly honored and maintained.

PROBLEM: One room sported bare concrete walls and the other wore a roughed-up coat of green that was more shabby than chic.

SOLUTION: : Kelli kept the green ceiling in the studio (it was in good shape) and gave the rest of the room a fresh, yellow wash. Next door, she opted for a neutral gray overall, with a red acrylic panel covering a window that connects the two rooms.

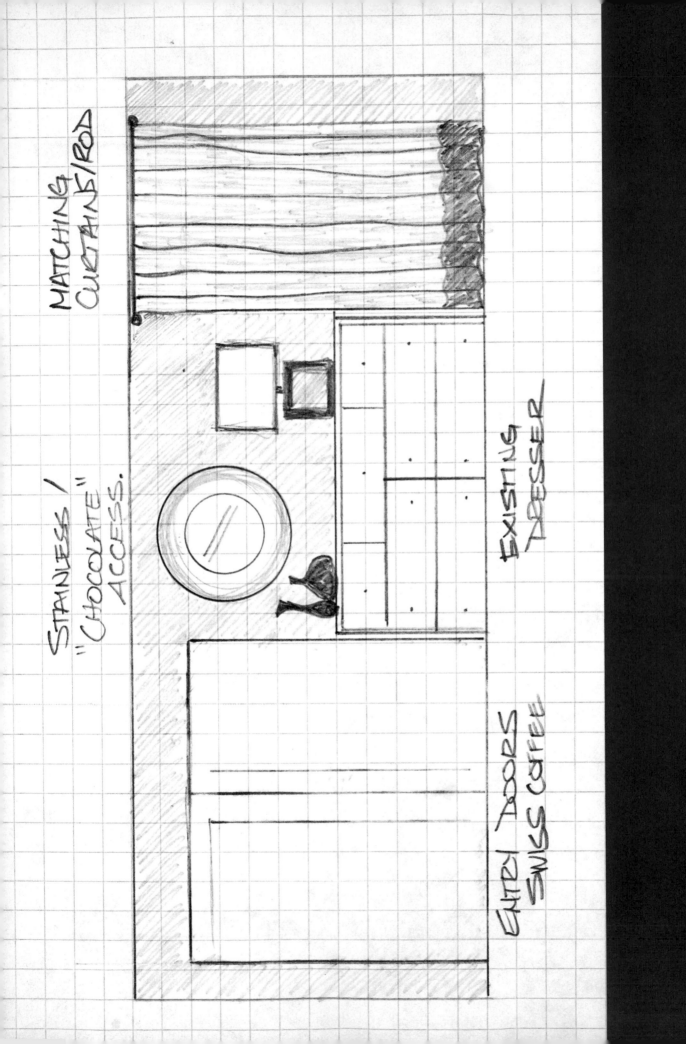

MATCHING CURTAINS/ROD

STAINLESS / "CHOCOLATE" ACCESS.

EXISTING DRESSER

ENTRY DOORS SWISS COFFEE

CHAPTER 11

LAYOUT TOOLS

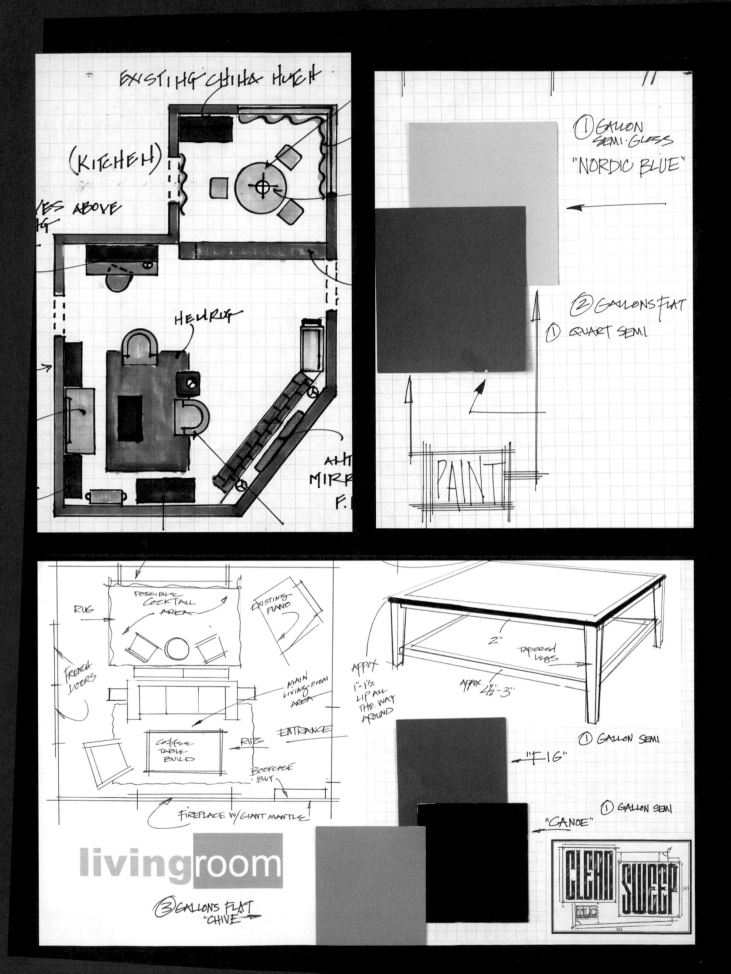

EXISTING CHINA HUTCH

(KITCHEN)

ES ABOVE

HELLRUG

AH
MIRR
F.

① GALLON
SEMI-GLOSS
"NORDIC BLUE"

② GALLONS FLAT
① QUART SEMI

PAINT

POSSIBLE
COCKTAIL
AREA

EXISTING
PIANO

RUG

FRENCH
DOORS

MAIN
LIVINGROOM
AREA

ENTRANCE

COFFEE
TABLE
BUILD

RUG

BOOKCASE
BUY

FIREPLACE W/ GIANT MANTLE

2" TAPERED LEGS

APPOX
1"-1½
LIP ALL
THE WAY
AROUND

APPOX 2½-3"

① GALLON SEMI

"FIG"

① GALLON SEMI

"CANOE"

living room

③ GALLONS FLAT
"CHIVE"

CLEAN SWEEP

"Space planning," says James, "is when you arrange furniture or map out a shelf system on paper before tackling the real thing. That way, you can see what will actually work before you get too far into any project." Sketch the details and you'll spare your floors, your walls, and your back. Use the grid on page 188 to plan your room and shelf systems. Here's how the *Clean Sweep* design team uses these tools:

STEP 1
Make multiple copies of pages 184–189 in black and white at a copy shop.

STEP 2
Measure your room and transfer its outline to the grid; one grid square equals 1 square foot of space. Mark openings (such as windows and doors) and architectural features (such as fireplaces and stairs), using the symbols *at right*.

STEP 3
Measure your keeper furniture and new furniture. Match them to the furniture pieces you copied from pages 184–187. Cut out the template furniture.

STEP 4
Arrange the room, consulting chapter 4 (pages 66–83) and chapter 5 (pages 84–109) for information on how to create zones and flow.

STEP 5
After you've settled on the desired layout, tape down the pieces and get to work!

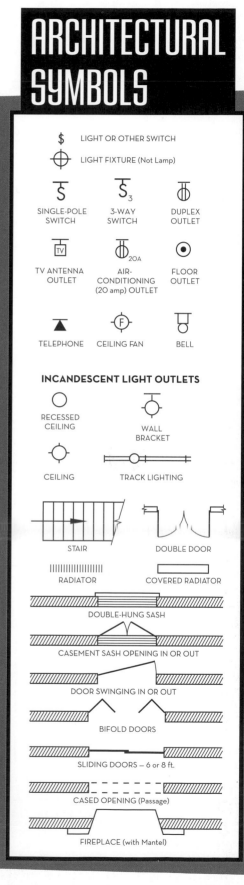

ARCHITECTURAL SYMBOLS

$ LIGHT OR OTHER SWITCH

LIGHT FIXTURE (Not Lamp)

SINGLE-POLE SWITCH · 3-WAY SWITCH · DUPLEX OUTLET

TV ANTENNA OUTLET · AIR-CONDITIONING (20 amp) OUTLET · FLOOR OUTLET

TELEPHONE · CEILING FAN · BELL

INCANDESCENT LIGHT OUTLETS

RECESSED CEILING · WALL BRACKET

CEILING · TRACK LIGHTING

STAIR · DOUBLE DOOR

RADIATOR · COVERED RADIATOR

DOUBLE-HUNG SASH

CASEMENT SASH OPENING IN OR OUT

DOOR SWINGING IN OR OUT

BIFOLD DOORS

SLIDING DOORS – 6 or 8 ft.

CASED OPENING (Passage)

FIREPLACE (with Mantel)

FURNITURE TEMPLATES

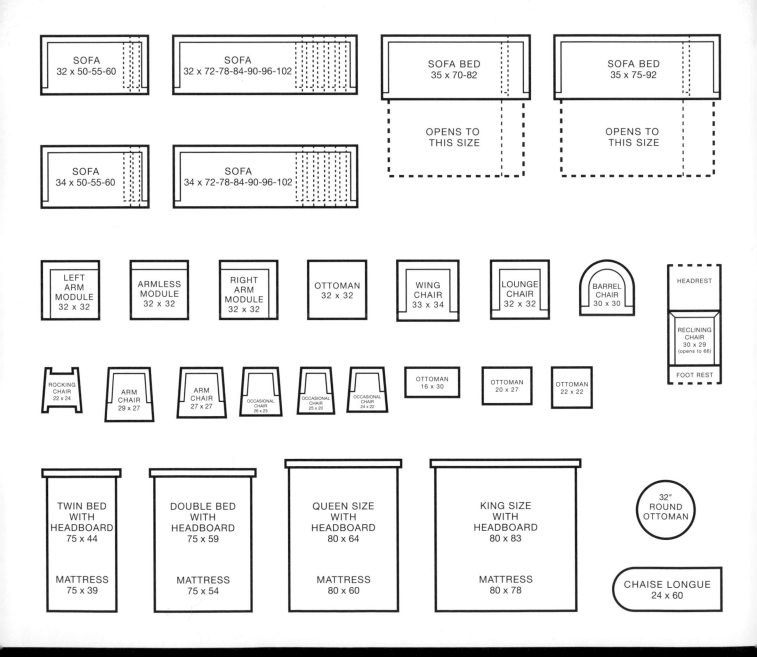

SOFA
32 x 50-55-60

SOFA
32 x 72-78-84-90-96-102

SOFA BED
35 x 70-82

OPENS TO
THIS SIZE

SOFA BED
35 x 75-92

OPENS TO
THIS SIZE

SOFA
34 x 50-55-60

SOFA
34 x 72-78-84-90-96-102

LEFT
ARM
MODULE
32 x 32

ARMLESS
MODULE
32 x 32

RIGHT
ARM
MODULE
32 x 32

OTTOMAN
32 x 32

WING
CHAIR
33 x 34

LOUNGE
CHAIR
32 x 32

BARREL
CHAIR
30 x 30

HEADREST

RECLINING
CHAIR
30 x 29
(opens to 66)

FOOT REST

ROCKING
CHAIR
22 x 24

ARM
CHAIR
29 x 27

ARM
CHAIR
27 x 27

OCCASIONAL
CHAIR
26 x 23

OCCASIONAL
CHAIR
25 x 20

OCCASIONAL
CHAIR
24 x 22

OTTOMAN
16 x 30

OTTOMAN
20 x 27

OTTOMAN
22 x 22

TWIN BED
WITH
HEADBOARD
75 x 44

MATTRESS
75 x 39

DOUBLE BED
WITH
HEADBOARD
75 x 59

MATTRESS
75 x 54

QUEEN SIZE
WITH
HEADBOARD
80 x 64

MATTRESS
80 x 60

KING SIZE
WITH
HEADBOARD
80 x 83

MATTRESS
80 x 78

32"
ROUND
OTTOMAN

CHAISE LONGUE
24 x 60

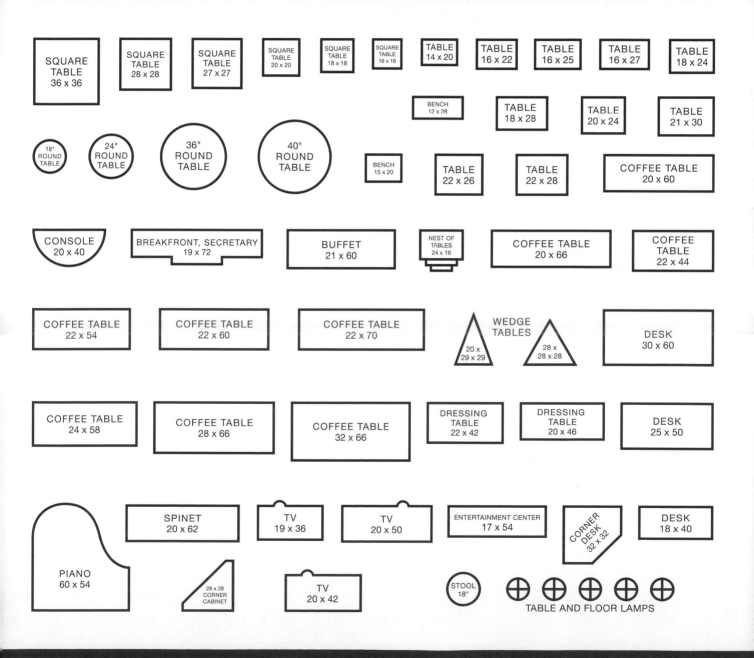

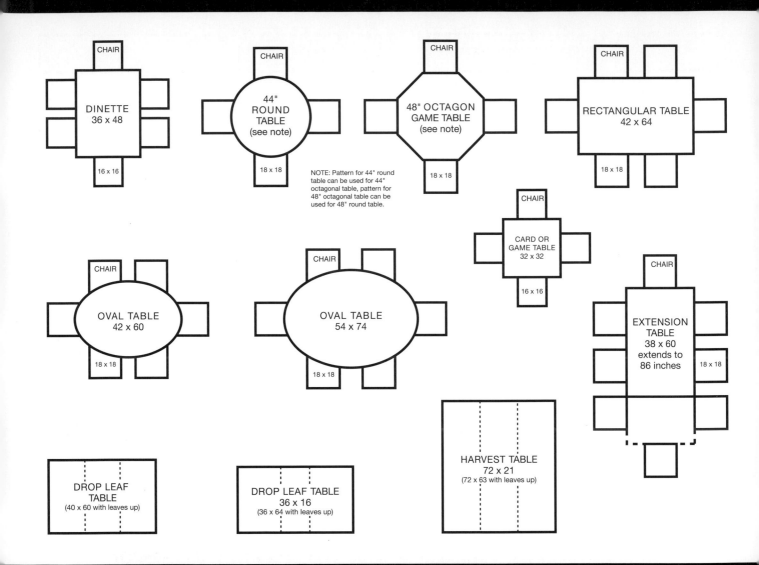

CHAIR

DINETTE
36 x 48

16 x 16

CHAIR

44"
ROUND
TABLE
(see note)

18 x 18

NOTE: Pattern for 44" round table can be used for 44" octagonal table, pattern for 48" octagonal table can be used for 48" round table.

CHAIR

48" OCTAGON
GAME TABLE
(see note)

18 x 18

CHAIR

RECTANGULAR TABLE
42 x 64

18 x 18

CHAIR

OVAL TABLE
42 x 60

18 x 18

CHAIR

OVAL TABLE
54 x 74

18 x 18

CHAIR

CARD OR
GAME TABLE
32 x 32

16 x 16

CHAIR

EXTENSION
TABLE
38 x 60
extends to
86 inches

18 x 18

HARVEST TABLE
72 x 21
(72 x 63 with leaves up)

DROP LEAF
TABLE
(40 x 60 with leaves up)

DROP LEAF TABLE
36 x 16
(36 x 64 with leaves up)

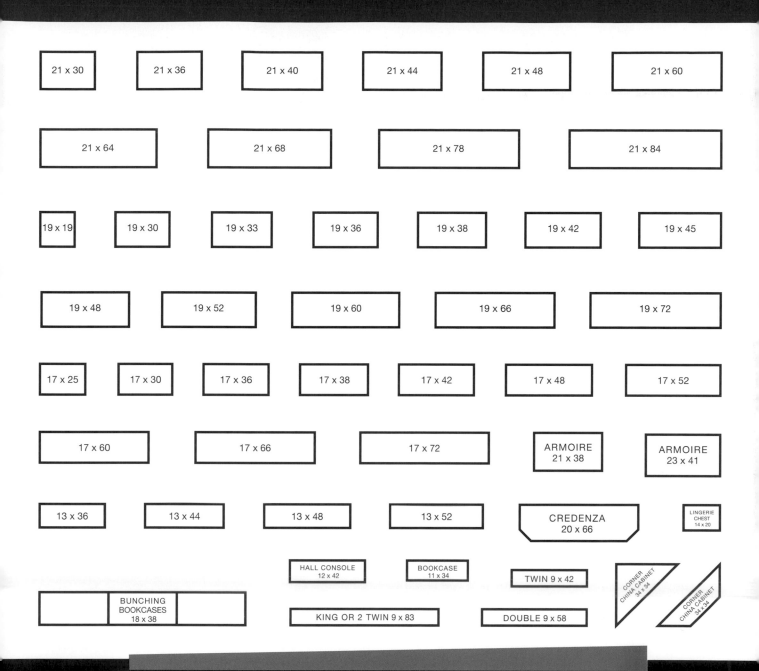

21 x 30 21 x 36 21 x 40 21 x 44 21 x 48 21 x 60

21 x 64 21 x 68 21 x 78 21 x 84

19 x 19 19 x 30 19 x 33 19 x 36 19 x 38 19 x 42 19 x 45

19 x 48 19 x 52 19 x 60 19 x 66 19 x 72

17 x 25 17 x 30 17 x 36 17 x 38 17 x 42 17 x 48 17 x 52

17 x 60 17 x 66 17 x 72 ARMOIRE 21 x 38 ARMOIRE 23 x 41

13 x 36 13 x 44 13 x 48 13 x 52 CREDENZA 20 x 66 LINGERIE CHEST 14 x 20

HALL CONSOLE 12 x 42 BOOKCASE 11 x 34 TWIN 9 x 42 CORNER CHINA CABINET 34 x 34 CORNER CHINA CABINET 34 x 34

BUNCHING BOOKCASES 18 x 38 KING OR 2 TWIN 9 x 83 DOUBLE 9 x 58

"YEARS OF LIVING IN STUDIOS FORCED ME TO FIND CREATIVE WAYS OF DEALING WITH A... [LIMITED] AMOUNT OF SPACE. I MOVED AND REARRANGED THINGS MONTH AFTER MONTH UNTIL I SETTLED ON THE BEST FLOOR PLAN. ONE THING I LEARNED? EVERYTHING HAS TO HAVE MULTIPLE FUNCTIONS."

A

Accessories, 90, 132–33
Amusement rooms, 102–9, 120–21
Assessment, of clutter situation, 30–39

B

Basement office, 178–79
Bedrooms
    assessment of, 32–33
    examples of, 92–97, 116–17, 130–31, 156–59, 174, 176
Behavioral patterns, tips for changing, 172
Behind-the-scenes photos, 22–23
Bike rack, 151
Bills, 165
Books and bookshelves, 76–77, 127, 164
Budgeting process, 91

C

Cast biographies, 8–21
CDs, 167
Charities, donations to, 60, 62
Children
    involvement of, 145
    playrooms for, 98–101, 120–21, 175
    toys, 164
Cleaning, 114
Closets
    in bedrooms, 130–31
    chalkboard painted doors for, 81
    clothes in, 163
    curtained doors for, 156, 158–59
    desks in, 127
    in offices, 81, 128
    planning of, 71

Clothes
    closet organization, 163
    folding tips, 145
    "live in the now" lesson, 172
Clutter
    costs of, 35
    "letting go," 171–72
    rules to live by, 166
    vs. mess, 30
Collectibles, 167
Color, choosing, 88
Compromises, 173
Containers, for storage, 143–145
Contracts, 173
Craft spaces, 34, 119, 164

D

Design, of space
    dictates, 87–91
    planning process, 69–70
Designers, biographies of, 14–21. See also specific designers
Desks, 75, 82–83, 127, 129
Diagram, of room, 69
Dining area, 74
Dream rooms, imagining, 43
Dust test, 51
DVDs, 167

E

Ellis, Kelli, 18–19, 62, 69, 70, 90, 130, 131, 143, 178–179

F

Financial records, 53, 165
Fireplaces, 75

Flaws, hiding of, 87
Folding tips, for clothes, 145
Function of room, determination of, 69
Furniture
    arrangement of, 70, 87, 183
    for bedrooms, 130–31
    do-it-yourself projects, 76–77, 127
    multifunctional pieces, 107
    for offices, 128–29
    what to keep, 125

G

Garages, 150–55
Garage sales, 57–63
Guest bedrooms, 176

J

Junk drawers, 166
Junk mail, 165

K

Keepers
    furniture, 125
    organization of, 48
    quiz for determining, 47

L

Laundry rooms, 134–37
Lighting, 87
Living areas
    assessment of, 36–37
    examples of, 37, 72–77, 89, 177
Love seat, with built-in bookshelf, 76–77
Luetkemeyer, Molly, 14–15, 62, 87, 91, 116–117, 125, 145, 151, 157, 176, 177

M

Mail, 165
Measurement, of room, 69
Medical records, 53
Memorabilia, 167, 171–72
Money-saving tips, 91
Monogrammed pillow, 132–33
Mood, 87, 88
Motivation, 172

O

Offices
    assessment of, 34–35
    examples of, 35, 75, 78–83,
    118–19, 128–29, 146–49,
    178–79
Organizational systems, 44, 48

P

Paint and painting, 113–21
    examples, 116–21
    how much to buy, 113
    preparation for, 113
    primer, 114
    process, 114
    show secrets, 115
Paperwork, what to keep, 53
Partners, working with, 48, 173
Photos, storage of, 167
Piles, for sorting purposes, 46–47
Pillow, monogrammed, 132–33
Planning process, 43–44, 183
Playrooms, 98–101, 120–21, 175
Pricing, of yard sale items, 58
Primer, 114
Purging, 43

Q

Quizzes
    Do you need a *Clean Sweep*?, 31
    for "keepers," 47

R

Records, guidelines for keeping, 53
Rec rooms, 102–9, 120–21

S

Saavedra, James, 20–21, 69, 88, 99,
    101, 118–119, 183
Sales, planning and holding, 57–63
Scrapbooking, 119, 164
Sell pile, 47
Shelf systems, 71, 144–45, 148–49
Shoes, 166
Signs, for yard sales, 57
Smiley, Tava, 8–9, 60, 61, 62
Sorting steps
    letting go of clutter, 171–72
    process, 43–53
    tips for, 46, 50–51
    tool kit for, 44
Space planning, 43–44, 183
Storage, 143–59. *See also* Closets
    analysis of, 70
    containers for, 143, 144
    for photos, 167
    for shoes, 166
    stacked storage unit, 108–9
    tips for, 143–45
    tool kit for, 145
    for toys, 164
Stromer, Eric, 12–13, 62, 126
Style, finding personal, 91
Surmelis, Angelo, 16–17, 87, 88,
    93, 95, 96, 113, 115, 125, 129,
    135, 147, 174, 175

T

Tables
    for laundry room, 134, 136–37
    with shelf, 154–55
Tax records, 53
Teenagers, bedroom for, 92–97
Time, finding for organization, 49
Time limits, 46
Tool bench, 150
Tool kits
    organization and storage, 145
    painting, 113
    shelf systems, 71
    sorting, 44
    yard sale, 58
Toss pile, 47
Toys, 164
Trash, 47, 52

V

Videotapes, 167

W

Wallpaper removal, 115
Walls, using for storage, 143
Walsh, Peter, 10–11, 30, 43, 48,
    62, 69, 143–44, 171, 172
Window treatments, 91
Work spaces. *See also* Offices
    assessment of, 38–39
    examples of, 75, 150

Y

Yard sales, 57–63

Z

Zones, in space planning process, 44